联合国教科文组织世界遗产中国项目研究
世界遗产与文化景观·数字档案系列
Research Projects on UNESCO World Heritage in China
World Heritage and Cultural Landscapes — Digital Documentation Series

GARDEN HERITAGE DIGITAL DOCUMENT
Heyuan Garden / Yangzhou

数字化园林遗产图录
扬州何园

杨晨　[澳]李·夏特　著
Yang Chen　Leigh Shutter

同济大学出版社
Tongji University Press

目 录
CONTENTS

01	系列概述 Overview of the Series	8
02	序言 Foreword	12
03	记录和表现场所 Recording and Representing Place	18
04	数字化园林遗产图录计划 Garden Heritage Digital Document Project	38
05	何园概况 Heyuan Garden Profile	52
06	何园历史沿革 Heyuan Garden History	56
07	何园整体特征 Heyuan Garden Character	68
08	园居院落 Residential Yards	84
09	西园 West Garden	110
10	东园 East Garden	146
11	片石山房及其他区域 Small-Rock Mountain Retreat and Other Precincts	180
12	附录 Appendix	208

01 系列概述
Overview of the Series

第四次工业革命速度之快、范围之广、程度之深前所未有，数字化技术在思想和思维等领域掀起了革命性的变化，不断满足和深化人类探索的欲望，深刻地影响着我们的认知方式、时空观和价值观。数字化技术正在带领我们穿越历史时空，无限接近和还原历史事实并畅想未来。

数字档案是指利用当代数字技术对自然和文化遗产的构成、历史、现状和使用情况等信息开展采集、分析、存储及发布工作，是遗产研究和保护的基石，也是当前国际文化遗产研究领域的最前沿。2003年，联合国教科文组织发布了《保存数字遗产宪章》，进一步拓展了我们对遗产的理解，使以数字方式生成或从现有资源转换成数字形式的文化和信息作品进入遗产行列。从这个意义上来说，自然和文化遗产的数字化记录，包括数据库、文字、图像，它们不仅是用于遗产保护管理的重要的档案文件，而且数字化档案本身就是一种新的数字遗产，将为人类知识的探索、储存、创造、交流和共享，提供广阔的前景。

文化景观反映人与自然之间的深刻互动及其结果，1992年联合国教科文组织将文化景观遗产定义为"自然与人类的共同作品"，并设有三个子类：人类有意设计和建造的景观、有机进化的景观和关联性景观。因为文化景观涉及自然和文化两大复杂系统，三个子类空间尺度和形式又存在较大差异，且常处于动态演进之中，故而文化景观遗产数字档案的建立，不仅需要技术支持，更需要从理论上确立遗产价值体系和对象，并充分反映在数据库结构及关键数据采集上。这项工作，在国内外，都是一个急需填补的空白点。

2010年中国大运河申遗，我应扬州申遗办邀请，主持"扬州瘦西湖文化景观价值"部分，其间开始组织对扬州瘦西湖文化景观进行全面的数字化档案探索。经过不间断

The 4th Industrial Revolution is unprecedented in speed, scope and depth. Digital technology has brought a revolutionary impact on our thoughts and thinking, constantly satisfying and deepening the desire of human exploration. It has also profoundly affected our cognition, views on time and space, and our values. Digital technology brings us on a journey in time and space, which enables us to ebulliently approach and rebuild historical circumstance and re-imagine the future.

Digital documentation refers to the use of contemporary digital technologies to collect, analyse, store, and publish information on the composition, history, current status, and usage of natural and cultural heritage. It is the new cornerstone of heritage research and conservation, and is also at the forefront of international cultural heritage research. The adoption of the *Charter on the Preservation of Digital Heritage* by UNESCO in 2003, expanded the concept of heritage to encompass cultural works and informational products either created digitally, or converted into digital form. In this sense, the digital records of natural and cultural heritage, including databases, texts, and images, are not only important documents for heritage conservation and management, but also a new type of digital heritage. This heritage brings human beings great opportunities to explore, store, create, communicate and share knowledge.

The cultural landscape reflects the profound interactions between humans and nature, and those outcomes. In 1992, UNESCO defined the cultural landscape heritage as 'the combined works of nature and of man', and it has three subcategories: the clearly defined landscape, the organically evolved landscape and the associative cultural landscape. Since the cultural landscape involves two complex systems of nature and culture, the spatial scale and form of the three subcategories are very different, and they are often in dynamic evolution. Therefore, the establishment of a digital documentation for cultural landscape heritage requires not only technical support, but also theories on heritage value systems and objects, which need to be fully reflected in the database structure and key data collection. This work is a gap that needs to be filled urgently both at home and abroad.

In 2010, invited by the Yangzhou World Heritage Application Office, I hosted the Research on Cultural Landscape Values of Slender West Lake in Yangzhou, and started to explore a digital documentation approach for the Slender West Lake cultural landscape. After continuous exploration and practice, in 2017, Yang Chen and I convened the Digital Cultural Landscape Working Group within the ICOMOS-IFLA International Scientific Committee on Cultural Landscapes to promote related work at the international frontier of the UNESCO World Heritage Cultural Landscape.

In the World Heritage and Cultural Landscape — Digital Documentation Series, the authors intend to present the latest research progress and outcomes of digital documentation for heritage via using the latest digital technology, selecting representative cultural landscape heritage sites such as classical gardens, rural landscapes, and historical urban landscapes in China, collecting digital heritage information and constructing databases according to different cultural landscape categories. The findings will be applied to the recognition, management, interpretation, exhibition and research of cultural landscape heritage. *Garden Heritage Digital Document: Heyuan Garden / Yangzhou* by Yang

的探索和实践，2017年我和杨晨在国际文化景观科学委员会召集成立了"数字文化景观"工作组，在联合国教科文组织世界遗产文化景观国际前沿推进相关工作。

"世界遗产与文化景观·数字档案系列"的作者团队希望通过应用最新数字技术，选取中国古典园林、乡村景观、城市历史景观等具有代表性的文化景观遗产，采集数字化遗产信息并分类建构数字化遗产数据库，以向公众展示数字化遗产档案的最新研究成果和进展。相关成果将应用于文化景观遗产的认知、管理、诠释、展示和研究交流。《数字化园林遗产图录：扬州何园》是该系列的第一本专著。希望有更多的学者加入这个系列的研究工作，共同推进中国和国际文化景观遗产数字档案工作的标准建设和体系化。

同济大学建筑与城市规划学院景观学系系主任，教授
2019年12月20日

Chen and Leigh Shutter is the first book in this series. I hope that more scholars will join the research for this series to promote the establishment of the standard and system for cultural landscape digital documentation in China and the rest of the world.

Han Feng
Professor, Director of Landscape Architecture Department, College of Architecture and Urban Planning, Tongji University

20 December 2019

02 序言 Foreword

扬州何园的保护和数字化管理

同济大学建筑与城市规划学院景观学系的杨晨老师与澳大利亚格里菲斯大学李·夏特副教授历时一年，寒来暑往、不辞辛劳，奔波于中国上海、扬州以及澳大利亚昆士兰州布里斯班市之间，顺利完成扬州何园数字化测绘工作。工作完成后，他们拟将研究成果出版，以便这一数字化成果可与社会各界分享。作为扬州何园的管理者，我认为这是一件可喜可贺的大事、好事。因此，当杨晨老师提出请我为本书写序时，我欣然应允。

扬州何园是在始建于清代康熙年间盐商吴家龙宅园的基础上修建的大型私家园林。清代康乾时期，扬州是两淮盐业生产、贸易、运输、管理中心，大批盐商聚集扬州，建造了不少精美的园林。《扬州画舫录》引清人刘大观语称："杭州以湖山胜，苏州以市肆胜，扬州以园亭胜。"甚至有人认为"扬州园林之胜，甲于天下""扬州城中园林之美甲于南中"等。何园所在的扬州南河下一带，由于靠近大运河，盐商纷纷选择在此居住，这里高屋连宇，园林成群。尽管何园最终建成于清代光绪年间，但由于园主人有较高的文化素养，加之扬州优渥的园林文化传承，以致何园建成后赢得"咸同后城内第一名园"的美誉。著名园林专家童寯指出："（何园）为扬州最大且最著名之私家园林，其规模以及营造技艺，堪与苏州园林媲美。"何园假山奇绝苍古，复廊回环纵横，建筑中西合璧，格局博大宏畅，造园手法推陈出新，在中国古典园林中有着独特的地位。1988年，国务院公布何园为全国重点文物保护单位。2013年，国家文物局将扬州何园列为中国大运河世界遗产的预备遗产点。

The conservation of Heyuan Garden and the digital management

Dr. Yang Chen, from the Department of Landscape Architecture, College of Architecture and Urban Planning, Tongji University, and Associate Professor Leigh Shutter from Griffith University in Australia, spent a year, travelling in the cold winter and hot summer between Shanghai, Yangzhou, and Brisbane, to complete the digital survey of Heyuan Garden. When the survey was finished, they edited the outcomes into a book for publication by Tongji University Press in order to share this digital result with the public. As a manager of Heyuan Garden, I think this is a great achievement. Therefore, when Dr. Yang Chen asked me to write this foreword, I was very pleased to accept.

Heyuan Garden in Yangzhou is a large private garden built to be the home of Wu Jialong, a salt merchant in the Kangxi reign of the Qing dynasty. During the Kangxi and Qianlong reigns, Yangzhou was the centre of the production, trade, transportation, and management of the salt industry on the northern and southern sides of the Huaihe River. A large number of salt merchants gathered in Yangzhou and built many beautiful gardens. *Yangzhou Huafang Lu* (The record of the painted pleasure boats of Yangzhou) quoted Liu Daguan saying in the Qing dynasty: 'Hangzhou puts its name on the map with its lakes and mountains, and Suzhou does so with its markets and shops, whereas Yangzhou excels with its gardens.' Some even think that 'gardens in Yangzhou are the best in China' and 'gardens in the city of Yangzhou are the best in the southern China' and so on. Heyuan Garden is located in the Nanhexia district (the southeast of Yangzhou City in the Qing dynasty). During that period, many salt merchants chose to live in this area as it was close to the Grand Canal. Many private gardens and buildings were created as a result. Heyuan Garden however, was finally completed during the Guangxu reign of the Qing dynasty due to the high cultural literacy of the owner and the inheritance of the outstanding garden culture in Yangzhou. Heyuan Garden won the reputation of 'the first garden in the city after the Xianfeng and Tongzhi reigns'. The famous garden expert Tong Jun pointed out: 'Heyuan Garden is the largest and most famous private garden in Yangzhou, and its scale and construction techniques are comparable to Suzhou gardens.' In Heyuan Garden, the rockeries are peculiar and antique, the corridors are winding and crisscross, the buildings are a combination of Chinese and Western styles, the garden structure is magnificent, and the gardening techniques are innovative. These qualities gave Heyuan Garden a unique position in Chinese classical gardens. Heyuan Garden was announced as a National Key Cultural Relics Protection Heritage Unit by the State Council in 1988. China's National Cultural Heritage Administration listed Heyuan Garden as a tentative heritage site for the Grand Canal World Heritage in 2013.

Protecting, inheriting, and making appropriate use of Heyuan Garden is an inescapable responsibility of the management team. Since Heyuan Garden first opened to the public in October 1959, the Management Office has always adhered to the Protection First principle. However, Heyuan Garden's conservation still faces multiple pressures and challenges, mainly manifested by increased protection pressure caused by tourism and excessive commercialisation, relatively insufficient protection funds, outdated protection methods, and lack of

保护、传承、妥善利用好扬州何园是其管理者不可推卸的责任。从1959年10月何园首次对外开放以来，何园管理处一直坚持"保护第一"的工作方针。但是，何园保护工作依然面临多重压力和挑战，主要表现为旅游及过度商业化带来的保护压力加大、保护经费相对不足、保护方法陈旧、保护专业人才缺乏等。总之，我们需要做的工作很多。让我感到欣喜的是同济大学建筑与城市规划学院能够青睐何园，将何园列入"数字化园林遗产图录"计划，对其开展数字化三维测绘工作，全面、完整、科学地展现何园的特征和价值，为何园的有效保护插上数字化的"翅膀"。同济大学此项开创性的研究工作让何园在私家园林文化景观遗产保护方面，率先露了一次"小荷"的"尖尖角"，诚不胜感激也！

是为序。

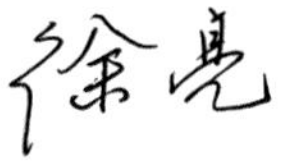

徐亮

扬州何园管理处负责人

2019年12月8日

protection professionals. In short, we need to do a lot of work. I am very pleased that the College of Architecture and Urban Planning of Tongji University has chosen Heyuan Garden and included it in the Garden Heritage Digital Document (GHDD) project, carrying out the digital 3D survey. This project will more comprehensively, completely and scientifically identify and present the characteristics and value of Heyuan Garden, which will eventually facilitate and improve the conservation and management of the garden. This groundbreaking research work by Tongji University has enabled Heyuan Garden to take the lead in the modern conservation practice of classical garden cultural landscapes. We really appreciate the team and the researchers.

This is the foreword I wrote for this book.

Xu Liang
Director of the Management Office of Heyuan Garden, Yangzhou
8 December 2019

1 《富春山居图》(《剩山图》部分)，黄公望，1347—1351年，现藏于浙江省博物馆
Dwelling in the Fuchun Mountains (*The Remaining Mountain* scroll), Huang Gongwang, 1347–1351, Zhejiang Provincial Museum in Hangzhou

03 记录和表现场所
Recording and Representing Place

每个灵魂都会为自己建造一座房子，房子之外是个世界，世界之外是个天堂。因此，这个世界为你而存在：建造属于你的世界。

——拉尔夫·沃尔多·爱默生

笛卡尔、波普尔和内格尔

我们理解并联系外部世界的过程是通过感知和认知能力调节的。我们因身体和思想而存在，同时又生活在物理空间中并与其互动。人类始终以一种独特而具体的视角向外看，这种观察方式受到物理宇宙环境以及各种要素的限制。每个人都是生命的"主体"，具有内在的主观体验；但同时我们也是客观物理世界的一部分，即"客体"。这是"所有期望并有能力超越特定视点来感知整体世界的生物都必须面对的问题"（内格尔，1986）。人类一直在

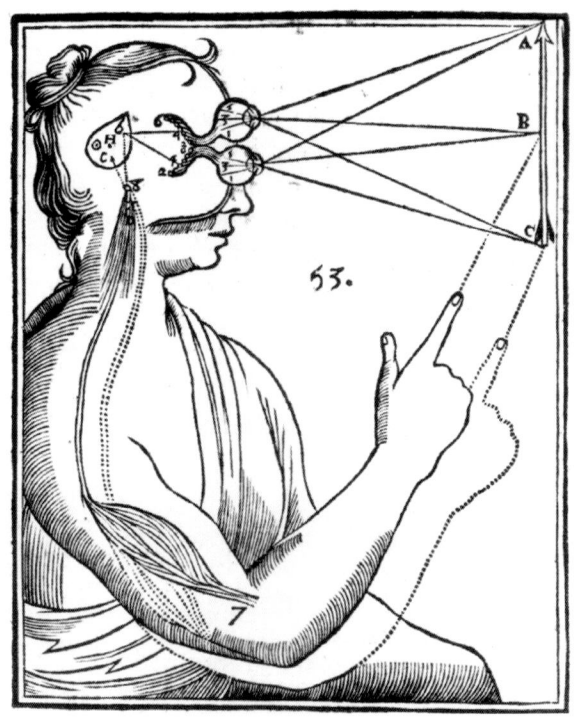

2 勒内·笛卡尔在《人类论》中绘制的视觉原理图，1677年. 来源：埃弗雷特收藏，公共领域
Theory of vision from René Descartes' *De Homine* (Treatise on Man), 1677. Source: The Everett Collection, public domain

Every spirit builds itself a house; and beyond its house, a world; and beyond its world a heaven. Know then, that the world exists for you: build, therefore, your own world.

— Ralph Waldo Emerson

Descartes, Popper and Nagel

Our relationship and understanding of the world in which we exist is mediated through our perceptual and cognitive faculties. Our mind and body become our being, but we engage with the objects and inhabit the space of an external physical world. We are outward looking, with a particular and unique perspective, yet are bound by the parameters and circumstance of a physical universe. As individuals we are the 'subject' of our lives, beings who have internalised subjective experience, but also part of the 'object', an external objective physical world. Making sense of this circumstance 'is a problem that faces every creature with the impulse and the capacity to transcend its particular point of view and to conceive of the world as a whole' (Nagel, 1986). This question of 'subject' and 'object' is a problem we have pondered and our musings, reflections and analysis recorded since the first Greek philosophers contemplated this question.

The French philosopher René Descartes in the 17th century described the world in terms of 'thought' and 'extension'. In his belief system and philosophical works, the subjective world of 'thought' was the essence of the mind, and all that we could truly know, the physical world, the world of matter, was the 'extension', that which must exist by reason. Descartes' Mind-Body Dualism laid the foundation for ongoing critical enquiry examining our place and relationship to the world. It continues to significantly influence Western philosophers.

Karl Popper, in his 1978 Tanner Lecture on human values, titled 'Three Worlds' re-conceives Descartes' Dualism by positing that rather than two, three worlds are the underpinning framework of our lives.

1 'There is, first, the world that consists of physical bodies, of stones and stars, of plants and animals, but also of radiation and other forms of physical energy. I will call this physical world, "world 1". '
2 'There is, secondly, the mental or psychological world, the world of our feelings of pain and of pleasure, of our thoughts, of our decisions, of our perceptions and our observations; in other words, the world of mental or psychological states or processes, or of subjective experiences. I will call it "world 2". '
3 The third is 'the world of the products of the human mind, such as languages; tales and stories and religious myths; scientific conjectures or theories, and mathematical constructions; songs and symphonies; paintings and sculptures. But also aeroplanes and airports and other feats of engineering...'(Popper, 1978). This is what Popper labels 'world 3'. What Popper also recognises is that these worlds while conceptually having different characteristics are not easily separated from each other in our daily lives.

This conception also adds the dimension of a collective and shared human understanding to Descartes' Dualism and perhaps better fits with lived experience.

Another key contemporary philosopher, Thomas Nagel, further builds on this conception in his 1986

思索关于"主体"和"客体"的问题，从第一位古希腊哲学家开始，我们的思辨和分析都被记录了下来。

17世纪法国哲学家勒内·笛卡尔用"思想"和"扩延"来描述世界。在他的认知体系和哲学著作中，"思想"的主观部分是思想的本质，而我们所能认知的物质世界是一种"扩延"，必须是理性存在的。笛卡尔的身心二元论为我们探讨场所以及人与世界的关系奠定了基础，并对西方哲学家产生了持续而重要的影响。

1978年，卡尔·波普尔发表了关于人类价值的题为"三个世界"的坦纳讲座，他重构了笛卡尔的二元论，认为我们生活的基础是三个世界，而不是两个。

第一，物理世界：世界由物质组成，包含石头、星星、动植物，还有辐射和其他形式的物理能量。这个物理世界可称为"世界一"。

第二，精神或心理世界：我们痛苦和愉悦的感觉，我们的思想、决定、立场和观察。换句话说，这是精神和心理状态、过程的世界，或者主观经验的世界。这个世界可称为"世界二"。

第三，人类思想产品世界，如语言、故事、宗教神话、科学猜想或理论以及数学建构、歌曲和交响曲、绘画和雕塑，此外还包含飞机、机场和其他工程技术的壮举（波普尔，1978）。波普尔将其称为"世界三"。波普尔还认识到，这些世界虽然在概念上具有不同的特征，但在生活中却密不可分。

波普尔的概念体系在笛卡尔二元论的基础上增加了人类共有思想的维度，这或许更接近生活经验。

另一位重要的当代哲学家托马斯·内格尔在1986年出版的专著《本然的观点》中进一步拓展了这一概念。他尝试"描述那些天生视角各异的复杂生物观察外部世界并在其中生活的方式"，并提出人类不能令人满意地统一主观与客观，这种尝试在本质上是不完整的，也是无法调和的。

以上讨论对记录和表现已知世界非常重要。对文化遗产而言，我们需要认识和理解其有形和无形的维度及特性，并通过有效的方法将它们传递给不同受众。这也是建筑师、风景园林师以及所有参与设计、建造、管理和分析建成环境的人员所必备的技能。我们需要记录、再现并重新构想世界，进而将相应的观点和知识传播出去。

许多当代学者认为，世界是内在联系的，脱离主观的客观世界并不存在，反之亦然。记录和再现世界的技术和工具也在不断发展，从人类早期在地表、岩石或木材表面做出的简单记号，到当代高度复杂的技术程序，每种手段都有其独特性，都被视为能更精准地表现特定的感知过程和实际经验。记录和再现是主观的，但同时也具有客观因素，即基于事实的科学描述，这也许更接近波普尔在"世界三"中的表述。回顾历史，我们发现人类在记录和表现环境的过程中，下意识地运用着不同的观点，有时偏向那些可以计量的、确切的特征，有时又希望表达更多的情感，或者直接采用传统的方法和手段。尽管当代科学强调客观的、无偏见的视角，我们仍不由自主地在表现过程和个人阐释中加入主观观念，并发掘和利用数据中所蕴含的其他特性。

以上观点可以帮助我们区分主观和客观，这对于探讨记录和再现物质世界的方法具有重要意义。具体而言，在最直接的感受层面，我们必须在空间中某个视点用肉眼观察世界。尽管我们能意识到视角带来的透视效果，也能推断外部环境的其他特征，但环境体验是随着时间而变化的，由一系列在时空变换中不断叠加的画面构成。

book *The View from Nowhere* (Nagel, 1986). In this work he proposes 'to describe a way of looking at the world and living in it that is suitable for complex beings without a naturally unified standpoint'. Nagel argues that we are unable to satisfactorily unify the two viewpoints, the subjective and objective, and that task is essentially incomplete and irreconcilable.

All this is important for recording and representing the world as we know it. It is important for cultural heritage to recognise and understand the qualities and dimensions of both the tangible and intangible, and to find ways to meaningfully communicate these qualities to different audiences. Indeed this is a fundamental skill required of architects, landscape architects and all those involved in the understanding, management, production and design of built environments, not just built cultural heritage: a capacity to record, represent and re-imagine the world and to coherently present that knowledge and those perspectives to others.

Many contemporary scholars see that these worlds are intrinsically associated, that there is no objective world without a subject and that vice versa, that there is no subject without an objective world. The tools and techniques involved in this conversation have also evolved over time, from the simplest markings on the earth, or on rock or timber surfaces made by early humans to highly sophisticated contemporary technological processes. Each of these techniques offers qualities and information that might be regarded as more closely representing an experiential, sensory account or interpretation, what we might regard as subjective, or perhaps a more factual scientific description, something more closely aligned with the objective, or indeed the understandings and conventions of Popper's 'world 3'.

Historically, we have, perhaps a little unconsciously, floated across these divisions, at times opting to emphasise the quantifiable and specific at others seeking to convey more emotion in our representations, or adopting other shared conventions of representation. While contemporary science demands an objective, unbiased perspective, we can equally see and relate to other qualities that are necessarily embedded in any data through the intrusion of the subjective, both in production and individual interpretation.

There are in this understanding some qualities that distinguish aspects of the subjective compared with the objective point of view, and these are particularly important when examining and contemplating our methods for recording and representing the physical world. Most particularly, at an immediate sensory level, we see the world through our eyes. We see the world, at any moment in time, from what is essentially a single point in space. While we see our view is perspectival and might understand and infer other properties of the environment, time does not stand still, and our experience is made up of an unfolding serial view of that external to us as we move through space and time. Our 'view' of the world is augmented by our extended sensory perceptual range: touch, sound, smell and taste. And that external world is constantly changing over time providing a dynamic sensory experience that is so much more than a single optical snapshot. Besides, we can describe and illustrate physical characteristics of the world that we can never quite perceive. Mathematics and other languages of science provide us with the means to describe and understand a world that remains elusive to our everyday perception.

感知能力的拓展强化了我们对世界的认知，包括触觉、听觉、嗅觉和味觉等。同时，不断变化的外部世界也为我们提供了动态的感受，这远远不是于某个单独视点所获得的"快照"能够捕捉的。此外，人类还能利用数学或其他科学手段描述和表达那些无法完全被感知的环境特征。例如，我们可以借助物理学和几何学创建正方形或立方体，但仅通过观察很难认识到它们所具有的几何尺寸和规律。透视往往会扭曲正方形的外观，导致从某个侧面看，正方形靠近视点的一侧比另一侧更长，与其相交的两条边则不平行。

为了理解并建造世界，包括建筑、住区和城市等，人类发明了各种方法来表现物质环境的特质。地图、平面图以及详尽完善的正投影技术能够始终如一地准确表达存在或可能存在的某种视角。正是在这一过程中，我们在不同程度上跨越了主体与客体的界限，也跨越了波普尔所提出的"三个世界"之间的差异。

创造记号和模型

制作于公元前6世纪的《巴比伦世界地图》（*Imago Mundi*）被认为是现存最早的世界地图。虽然今天无法看到该地图的原貌，但考古学家已经将碎片拼接完整并陈列在大英博物馆里。这块泥质的图版是对当时已知世界的描绘。它是对物理世界几何形态的再现，但也融合了对神话信仰的图示。通过观察这张地图，我们可以从本质上理解和解读它所描绘的内容以及它所记录的信息，这些信息证明了物理世界的一些持久的特征，以及在几千年中幸存下来的文化愿景。事实证明，记录和再现的过程必然无法清晰区分主观和客观，波普尔的"三个世界"在这过程中找到了各自的表达途径。

的确，当我们审视地图、平面图、剖面图、立面图、轴测图、透视图、照片、图表、草图等所有历史上出现过

的再现外部世界的手段和形式，不难发现，物理环境以及个人和集体的存在为这些活动提供了必要的基础。再现其实就像其他工作一样，无法脱离物理、个人和文化的维度，主观和客观是相互依存的。但历史上，我们常常不愿意承认这种不可分割的关系，或者说至少更愿意强调某个观点。在中世纪，等距投影的出现很好地迎合了客观的传统，并且提供了一种避免基于个人情感的表达方式。这种几何学手段超越了对透视的理解，并且广泛传播和应用于其他群体和文化当中。

3 《巴比伦世界地图》，描绘了亚述、巴比伦和亚美尼亚.
来源：大英博物馆藏品，公共领域
Imago Mundi. Map showing Assyria, Babylonia and Armenia.
Source: Collection of the British Museum, public domain

For example we know we can create objects that are square or cubic in shape; an understanding of physics and geometry enables us to achieve that outcome, but when as individuals we look at those objects, they don't appear to have the dimensions and regularity ascribed by the intrinsic mathematical geometry. The side of the square closest to the observer appears longer than that further away. Opposite edges don't appear parallel. The square's apparent shape is distorted by our perspective view.

To understand the natural and build our world, homes, settlements and cities, humankind has had to invent ways to codify qualities of the physical world. We have invented techniques and processes for making maps and plans. We have developed elaborate, conventionalised orthographic projection techniques that enable us to consistently and accurately communicate a view of what exists or what might exist. In these processes we transcend to varying degrees the differences between subject and object or Popper's Three Worlds.

Making marks and models

What is believed to be the earliest known and still existing world map is the *Imago Mundi* fabricated in Babylon in the 6th century BCE. We no longer have the complete undamaged original artefact but archaeologists have pieced together the fragments which now reside in the British Museum. This clay tablet has been interpreted as a depiction of the known world from the period. It is partially a geometric representation of the physical world, but is melded with the graphic depiction of mythical beliefs. That we are able to look at this map and still essentially understand and interpret what it depicts and the message it records is in itself a proof of the enduring characteristics of the physical world that we inhabit and the shared cultural prospect that has survived across millennia. The process of recording and representing is demonstrated to be necessarily one where subject and object cannot be clearly distinguished and where Popper's Three Worlds each find expression.

Indeed if we examine the maps, plans, sections, elevations, isometrics, axonometrics, perspectives, photos, diagrams, sketches: all the various stylised modes of representing the world across history, we are confronted by the unavoidable reality that any work engaged in this activity must find a basis in a physical, personal and collective existence. Representation, as with everything we do, cannot be without a physical, personal or cultural dimension. Subject and object are mutually dependent. Across history we have often not conceded this inseparable relationship, or have at least premiated the value of one point of view or another. In the middle ages the development of isometric projection grasped at the idea of an objective convention that offered a way of representation that eschewed the emotive and personal. This geometric convention of representation preceded the understanding of perspective and was developed and known widely by unrelated communities and cultures.

Similarly the construction and production of physical scale models offered a standard and degree of permanence to that being depicted, whether existing or imagined. Models were very much part of the physical world, reduced size replicas of the natural or built environment. Their three dimensional form enabled the viewer to observe them as if they were the real artefact or place. One could walk around them, perhaps even venture inside, witness them

4 《三国演义》插图,作者不详,15世纪,可见古人曾使用二维图形化的表达方式来呈现三维效果. 来源:北京大学藏品,公共领域
Illustration from *Romance of the Three Kingdoms*, illustrator unknown, 15th century, indicating that two dimensional graphic expression was once employed to give the impression of three dimensions. Source: Collection of Peking University, public domain

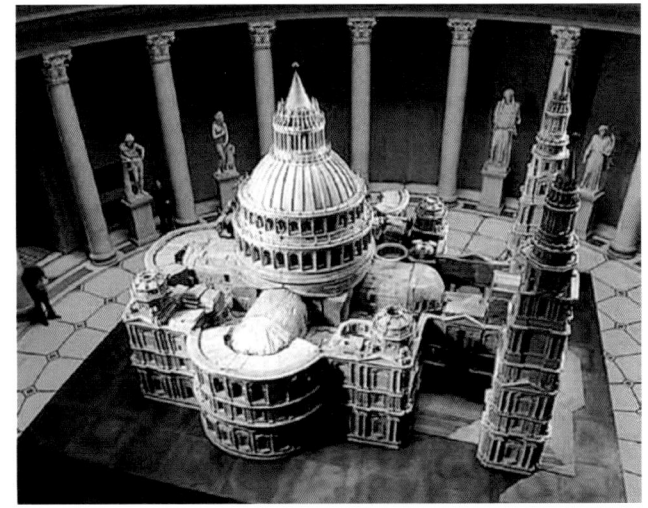

5 圣彼得大教堂设计方案木质模型,小安东尼奥·达·桑加洛设计,安东尼奥·拉巴科制作于1539—1543年. 来源:照片由大都会艺术博物馆提供,公共领域
Timber model of design proposal St. Peter's Basilica. Designed by Antonio da Sangallo the younger and built by Antonio Labacco, 1539–1543. Source: photo provided by Metropolitan Museum of Art, public domain

同样,对于现实或者想象中的环境来说,建造和制作等比例物理模型也为再现提供了一种标准和某种意义上的永久保存方式。在很大程度上,模型是物理世界的重要组成部分,是自然或建成环境的缩小副本。三维的形式使我们可以像观察真实环境一样审视它们,人们可以在周围移动,甚至可以进入,在不同场合、不断变化的自然环境和社交环境,以及不同的光照或天气条件下观察它们。三维模型是一种完全具象的复制,它模仿原物的形状和空间比例,但并不包含模式化的过程。建模是模拟物理或文化世界某些方面的常用和公认的方法,它以大多数二维表现无法实现的方式来促进对环境的理解和交流。毫无疑问,这种对世界的触觉感知交互方式比物理学或者透视几何理论出现的时间还要早。事实证明,创造一些可触、可见的物理模型比揭示和表达我们观察世界时下意识的心理过程要容易得多。一个复制品,或者说一种直接的模仿,即使尺寸较小,也是一个简单的理性飞跃。

长期以来,视觉一直是我们的主要感知途径,是生命体下意识的工作,这种活动几乎不可察觉,但却是我们与世界互动的核心途径。或许正因如此,也因为涉及那些复杂的生物物理过程,我们花了很长时间来揭示人类的观察和感知之间所蕴含的光学和几何特性。在15世纪早期,1415—1420年间,菲利波·伯鲁内列斯基开创了透视几何法,尝试以几何透视原理表现佛罗伦萨的建筑。在实验中,他依据推导出的几何原理绘制建筑图纸,展示了建筑物和城市环境的形貌,这一方法沿用至今。这项工作并非以一种更加客观和抽象的方式来表现世界,而是建立了一个过程,使艺术家能够更直接地参与并再现人类体验到的视觉感知,以观众观察现实世界

in different light or weather conditions on different occasions and in changing physical environments and social circumstance. The three dimensional form is not simulated or conventionalised. It imitates the shape and spatial proportions of the original. Model making remains a commonly understood and agreed process for simulating some aspect of the physical or cultural worlds. It facilitates understanding and communication in a way that most two dimensional representation fails to achieve. It is not surprising that this mode of tactile sensory engagement depicting the physical world developed ahead of understanding of the physics of vision and geometry of perspective. The capacity to create artefacts that are facsimiles of that we can touch and see proved easier than unravelling and transcribing the mental processes unconsciously taking place as we view the world. A copy, a direct likeness, even if smaller was a simpler intellectual leap.

Sight has long been our primary sense, a subconscious task of our very being, almost imperceptible but utterly central to our engagement with the world. Perhaps for this reason, and the extraordinary bio-physical processes involved it took so long to explain the optics and geometrical properties of the relationship of what we perceive and 'see' to what we view. It was not until between 1415 and 1420, in the early fifteenth century that Filippo Brunelleschi made an explanation of the geometry of perspective. In his experiments he made drawings of Florence's architecture using the geometric principles that he had developed to show these buildings and the urban environments in what we now regard as correct perspective. Rather than attempting to represent the world in a more objective and abstracted form, this work established a process to enable artists to more directly engage with and reproduce the visual perception of human experience, to record and show the world to an audience in the same way that the real world was seen by that audience. To demonstrate the veracity of this mode of representation, Brunelleschi would have a member of the public view a scene through a small hole in a screen, and would then place one of his artworks in front of the screen. To the observer the physical world and the artwork would appear to be the same. The geometry of the constructed image was seen to be identical to that of the real world.

The German artist Albrecht Dürer, was another who explored these processes. He experimented with the mathematics and physical properties of perspective, constructing devices to better understand and employ its attributes in his work. The invention of basic ray tracing technique is credited to Dürer. This technique and understanding of physics is now employed in modern computer graphics software and processes.

Between 1798 and 1801 Napoleon Bonaparte lead a military campaign in Egypt and Syria. The invading contingent of these forces of France surprisingly included a substantial survey party, a total of 167 scientists and scholars ('savants'), to record and document the wonders of this ancient world. The resources allocated to this venture and intellectual enterprise of discovery is often regarded as a demonstration of Napoleon's commitment to the principles of the Enlightenment. However, others brand it as hubris and propaganda hiding Bonaparte's underlying quest for territory and power. Regardless of motive one outcome was the publication of the extraordinary *Description de l'Égypte* compiled between 1809 and 1829. This series of volumes documenting the natural history of the country, its antiquities and modern characteristics aimed

的方式为他们记录和再现世界。为了证明这种再现方式的准确性,伯鲁内列斯基请观众通过屏幕上的小孔观看一处场景,然后将他自己对该场景的绘图放在屏幕前用于对照。对观察者来说,物理世界和图纸再现似乎是无差别的,伯鲁内列斯基所构造图像的几何形状被视为与真实世界一致。

德国艺术家阿尔布雷特·丢勒是另一位探索这些过程的先驱。他尝试剖析透视的数学和物理特性,构造了可以更好地理解和运用其属性的设备。丢勒发明了基本光线跟踪技术,直到今天,这种技术及其背后的物理原理仍旧为现代计算机图形软件所用。

1798年至1801年间,拿破仑·波拿巴领导了在埃及和叙利亚的军事行动。令人惊讶的是,入侵的法国部队拥有一支庞大的测绘团队,167名科学家和学者测绘和记录了这片古代世界的奇观。测绘团队获得了巨大的支持,有些人将其视为拿破仑对启蒙运动精神的追求,但也有人觉得这只是拿破仑渴望领土和权力的体现。不管最初动机如何,我们看到了一个意想不到的伟大成果——出版于1809年至1829年间的《埃及描述》(Description de l'Égypte)。该著作记载了埃及的自然历史、文物和现代特征,为所有经过测绘和研究的场所和材料提供了详尽说明。法国艺术家、陆军军官、机械天才尼古拉-雅克·孔特是这项庞大工作的主要贡

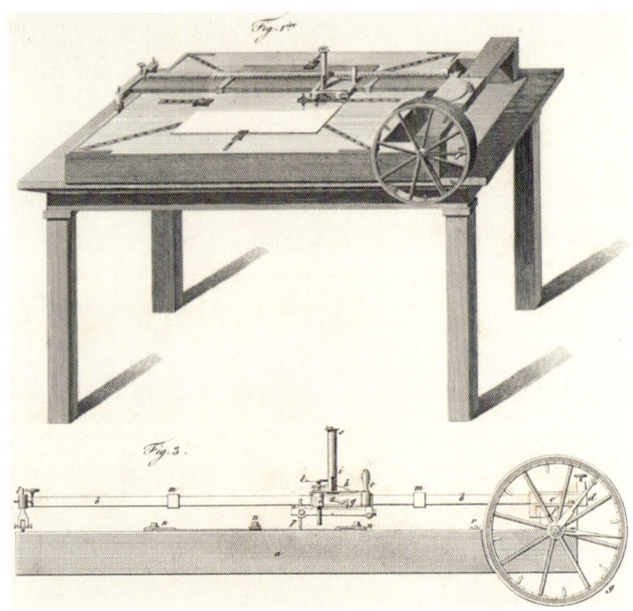

6 孔特的雕版机,摘自《埃及描述》或《法军远征期间在埃及收集的观察和研究》,1809—1829年. 来源:巴黎帝国印刷厂,公共领域
Conté's engraving machine, from *Description de l'Égypte*; or, *Recueil des observations et des recherches qui ont été faites en Égypte pendant l'expédition de l'armée française*, 1809–1829. Source: De L'Imprimerie impériale, Paris, public domain

7 版画,摘自《埃及描述》或《法军远征期间在埃及收集的观察和研究》,1809—1829年. 来源:巴黎帝国印刷厂,公共领域
Engraving, from *Description de l'Égypte*; or, *Recueil des observations et des recherches qui ont été faites en Égypte pendant l'expédition de l'armée française*, 1809–1829. Source: De L'Imprimerie impériale, Paris, public domain

to provide a comprehensive catalog of the materials and places surveyed and studied. A key contributor to this vast work was an artist, French army officer and mechanical genius Nicolas-Jacques Conté. The inventor of the modern pencil lead seemed able to contrive all manner of mechanical devices to support, and make more efficient the enormous undertaking. He was able to design, build models, organise and oversee the production process. On his return to France in 1802 he had been assigned to lead the team tasked with publishing the survey material. In this effort his most notable contribution was the invention of an engraving machine that substantially reduced production time and enabled the creation of exquisite, finely detailed prints depicting the discovered treasures. Conté died at the relatively early age of 50 in 1805 just as the project was taking shape. His contribution and legacy was never the less enormous, laying the foundations and developing the means to produce an enduring work of great beauty, depth and value.

Seeing beyond the scale of self

As we normally experience the world everything is at the scale of 1:1, the creatures, landscapes and objects that we encounter are at full size: no smaller or bigger. There are of course some big and some small things but that is how they naturally occur. The discovery of lenses, optical devices that transmit and refract light, changed this relationship. Here is a device that when used to view an object makes it appear bigger. Lenses offered the opportunity to see beyond the scale of self. Archeological evidence suggests that lenses may have been used in antiquity and that they have been employed across the millennia since. Reading glasses or spectacles, however were not invented until the second half of

8 阿尔布雷特·丢勒的木版画:《鲁特琴的制图员》, 约1600年.
来源: 大都会艺术博物馆, 公共领域
The Draftsman of Lute by Albrecht Dürer, woodblock print, ca 1600. Source: Metropolitan Museum of Art, public domain

the 13th century and it was only after a further three hundred years that more adventurous advanced applications were achieved.

The earliest known working telescopes are thought to have developed in the Netherlands in the early 17th century with microscopes being developed soon after. These optical instruments arranged together multiple lenses in a tubular frame, creating a device that could magnify that being observed. A famous early adopter and developer of the telescope was Galileo Galilei. He constructed his own device for observing celestial bodies, and in November 1609 viewed the Moon and made watercolour illustrations recording the Earth satellite in its various phases.

These depictions are the first detailed representations of the Moon in history. Galileo with this new device was able to see the moon in a way not previously possible.

献者。孔特作为现代铅笔芯的发明人，似乎能够设计各式各样的机械设备来提升测绘效率并支持这部伟大作品的出版。他设计和构建模型，并组织和监督制作过程。1802年回到法国后，孔特受命负责发布测绘成果，他最大的贡献是发明了一种雕版机，从而大大缩短生产时间，并且能够绘制精美且精细的图片来描绘发现的宝藏。但项目还没结束，孔特就在1805年逝世了，年仅50岁。孔特的贡献和遗产不容小觑，他的发明为制作出具有美感、深度和价值的再现作品提供了基础和关键手段。

超越自我尺度的观察

通常我们体验世界的比例是1：1。我们观察到的生物、风景和物体都是全尺寸的，即其实际尺寸，并未放大或缩小。当然，自然界中有或大或小的事物，但那都是自然的结果。作为一种透射和折射光的设备，透镜的出现改变了这种关系，它是一种用于观察对象的设备，可使观察的对象看起来更大，因此，镜头提供了超越自我尺度的机会。考古证据表明，透镜在古代世界很可能已被使用，并沿用了数千年。但老花镜或眼镜直到13世纪下半叶才出现，之后又过了300年才实现了应用升级。

据考证，已知最早的工作望远镜是17世纪初期在荷兰发明的，不久之后发明了显微镜。这些光学仪器将多个透镜布置在管状镜架中，构成了可以观察到放大效果的设备。伽利略·伽利莱是望远镜的早期开发者和使用者，他在1609年11月利用自创的天体观测装置观看月球，并制作了水彩插图记录了月球在不同时段的样子，它们是历史上第一次对月球的详细描绘。伽利略创造了一种全新的观察月球的方式。

今天，望远镜和太空旅行的出现让我们能更好地放大并观察宇宙中存在的事物或者观察地球本身。科学的发展

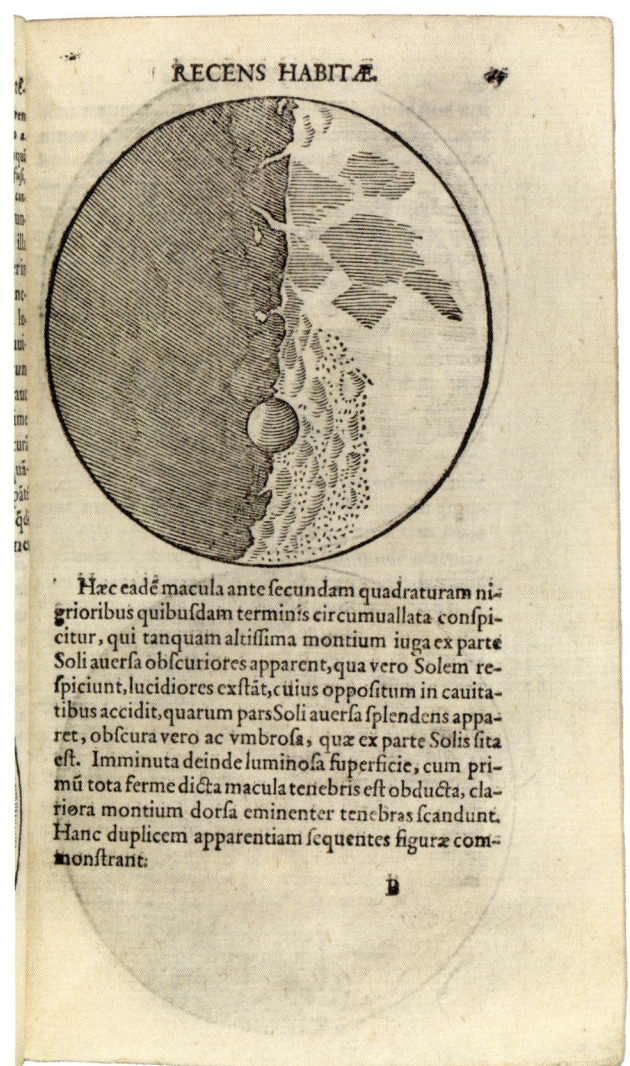

9 伽利略·伽利莱创作的月球视图，1610年发表于《星际信使》. 来源：帕多瓦大学博物馆，公共领域
Moon view by Galileo Galilei published in *Sidereus Nuncius*, 1610. Source: Museum of Università di Padova, public domain

使望远镜的设计越来越复杂，功能也越来越强大，人们可以向太空中看得更远。光学望远镜仍然是探索太空的重要设备，但射电天文学的发展进一步扩展了人类的探测范围。卡尔·詹斯基超大型天线阵（VLA）是位于美国新墨西哥州中部的射电天文台。VLA由28个单独的25米射电望远镜组成，可以在沙漠中来回移动，以不

Today's telescopes and the advent of space travel have provided even more opportunities to better magnify and see what is out there in the universe, or alternatively to direct our gaze back on the planet we inhabit. Science has produced telescopes with increasing sophistication and power enabling a view deeper and deeper into space. Optical telescopes remain an important device in the exploration of space, but the new science of radio astronomy gives us equipment that extends our reach. The Karl G. Jansky Very Large Array (VLA) is a radio astronomy observatory located in central New Mexico, USA. The VLA is made up of twenty-eight individual 25-metre radio telescopes which can be moved back and forth across the desert landscape to achieve different spacings and configurations for specific research. It can see millions of light years into the galaxy.

While telescopes have the visual effect of bringing objects that are far away closer to us, microscopes make little things that are quite close seem much bigger. Foremost among these instruments is the scanning electron microscope (SEM) invented in 1937. An SEM is a type of electron microscope that produces images of a sample by scanning the surface with a focused beam of electrons. The electrons interact with atoms in the sample, producing various signals that contain information about the surface topography and composition of the sample. The electron beam is scanned in a raster scan pattern, and the position of the beam is combined with the intensity of the detected signal to produce an image. A SEM can achieve resolution better than 1 nanometre.

Sunlight and shade, rain and wind, sound and smell

When the processes of photography were first discovered and photographs began to be taken and broadly distributed, it was thought that these images were capturing and reproducing reality. They were not as past artworks, drawings, prints and paintings, the unique product of a fanciful and creative mind that might on occasion choose to incorporate and imitate aspects of the world we see, but instead considered reproducible and authentic facsimiles. Susan Sontag noted in *On Photography* : 'In the fairy tale of photography the magic box insures veracity and banishes error, compensates for inexperience and rewards innocence.' This same mindset has permeated our contemporary embrace of the new technology and capability of 3D mapping techniques. Once again we are infected with enthusiasm and belief in the perceived verisimilitude of these processes and outputs. What we fail to register is the current paucity of record or capacity to reproduce lived experience, the qualities and feelings that provide the depth of engagement and connection to place. The full sensory encounter with environment or event, the sunlight and shade, rain and wind, sound and smell on our bodies and physical setting that contribute to the intensity of feeling, emotional immersion and indeed understanding.

Values, beliefs and shared knowledge

We are drawn together as communities by our shared values, beliefs, knowledge and understandings of the world. Our social disposition and capacity to communicate and live with each other relies on the connection and participation that each of us makes with this intangible shared world. This is Popper's 'world 3'. It provides us with an essential

同的间距和配置满足特定的实验需求，它可以看到数百万光年的星系。

望远镜可以让很远的物体看起来很近，显微镜则能使距离较近的小东西看起来更大。其中最重要的是1937年发明的扫描电子显微镜（SEM），通过用聚焦的电子束扫描表面来建立图像。电子与观测对象中的原子相互作用，产生各种信号，其中包含有关样品的表面形貌和成分的信息。电子束以光栅扫描模式进行测绘，电子束的位置与检测到的信号的强度结合以产生图像，从而实现优于1纳米的分辨率。

阳光和阴影，雨和风，声音和气味

当我们发明了摄影技术并且广泛使用照片的时候，我们认为这些图像正在捕捉和再现现实。之前采用的艺术品、素描、印刷物和绘画是幻想和创造力的独特产物，它们或许偶尔才会有选择地吸收和模仿可见世界的某些方面。但照片和它们不同，照片被认为是对于物体真实的复制。正如苏珊·桑塔格在《论摄影》中指出的那样："在摄影的神话中，魔术盒确保了准确性并消除了错误，弥补了经验不足并奖励了纯真。"这种观念已经渗透到我们今天对新技术和三维映射技术功能的巨大热情中，我们再次被这些过程及其真实感打动。但是，我们仍旧欠缺记录和再现活态经验及感受的能力，而这些往往反映着人与场所之间的深度互动和关联。身体的感官系统与光影、风雨、声音、气味等环境或事件要素的完整接触，对于强化我们的场所体验和情感沉浸并促进真正的理解而言，仍旧至关重要。

价值观、信念和共享知识

我们通过共享的价值观、信念、知识和对世界的了解而组成了社群。我们的社会性以及相互沟通和生活的能力取决于我们每个人与世界的联系和互动，这就是波普尔提出的"世界三"。"世界三"是我们建构共同认知框架的重要部分，使我们能够集体生活，能在主观和客观之间进行调节，也使艺术与科学的表达相互融合。由此文化得以向个人传播，并将个人与外部环境联系起来。

当人们观察世界并再现所看到的事物时，必然会接受自身所在群体的文化观点。通常，个人与群体之间的动态关系是伟大思想和艺术的催化剂。回溯人类再现环境的历史，尤其是希望通过再现以提供科学记录的历史，我们会发现这种情况并不鲜见。历史上出现了很多艺术家

10　美国新墨西哥州的卡尔·詹斯基超大型天线阵. 摄影: 迪克里昂, CC BY-SA 4.0
The Karl G. Jansky VLA, New Mexico, USA. Photo panorama by Dicklyon, CC BY-SA 4.0

part of the cognitive framework that enables us to live collectively. This is the world that mediates between the subjective and objective, where artistic and scientific expression merge. Where culture embraces the individual and connects that person with the physical.

When we look at the world and then represent what we see, we necessarily embrace the cultural perspectives of the communities in which we live. The dynamic intellectual relationship between individual and community is often the catalyst for great ideas and art. This is no less so when we look at a history of representations of physical environments and in particular those aiming to capture and embed a rich scientific record. There are very many artists and draftsmen to consider but by way of example for our purpose here we shall focus on the Dutch graphic artist M. C. Escher. He produced a range of intriguing works from the early to mid 20th century. In particular, he focused on the geometric conventions of two dimensional representation and visual perception creating many works incorporating impossible objects and perspectives. An impossible object is a form of optical illusion. In the illusion a two-dimensional figure is made to appear to represent a three dimensional object. Our visual system subconsciously interprets the image of the three dimensional geometry, assigning it properties that are impossible in the physical world. Escher's works are confounding. Compelling in their apparent veracity to reproduce the subject matter while at the same time presenting a completely distorted view of the world. Our attention to the competing perspectives of the subjective and objective could not be more sharply drawn in to focus.

Hermann von Helmholtz is often credited with the first study of visual perception in modern times. Helmholtz examined the human eye and concluded that it was incapable of producing a high quality image. Insufficient information seemed to make vision impossible. He therefore concluded that vision could only be the result of some form of 'unconscious inference', coining that term in 1867. He proposed the brain was making assumptions and conclusions from incomplete data, based on previous experiences.

We do not just 'see' the world, but create a world that hovers between an objective physical construct and one of experience and imagination. We have not always recognised the subjective patina that we apply to those representations of the world considered objective and authentic. In our maps we have for centuries unwittingly applied an invisible intellectual coding that renders the world in ways that conform to shared social and cultural practices and conventionalised techniques. Or perhaps pray on our subconscious intuitions to promote particular political, social and cultural perspectives.

Artists have long recognised and understood this circumstance and in more recent decades have become increasingly 'captivated by the entwinements of beauty and power, truth and artifice, and the fantasy and functionality they perceive in geographical mapmaking' (Ferdinand, 2019). 'Map Art' has become a defined domain of art activity and exploration. This field has been extensively investigated and analysed by Simon Ferdinand in *Mapping beyond Measure: Art, Cartography and the Space of Global Modernity*. In this treatise Ferdinand curates and explores a diverse range of map based artistic works that provide a perspective that extends

和制图家，荷兰的图形艺术家莫里兹·柯尼利斯·埃舍尔是其中之一。从20世纪初到20世纪中叶，埃舍尔专注于研究二维再现和视觉感知的几何原理，创作了一系列关于不可见物体和视角的有趣作品。不可见物体是一种视错觉，利用二维图形再现三维物体。我们的视觉系统会下意识地解释三维几何图形的图像，并赋予其在物理世界中不可能实现的特性。埃舍尔的作品令人费解，通过模拟表面的真实来再现对象，同时呈现出完全扭曲的视角，这清晰地反映了我们之前讨论的主观和客观相互竞争的问题。

赫尔曼·冯·亥姆霍兹被认为是近代视知觉研究第一人。亥姆霍兹检查了人眼，发现它无法产生高质量的图像，信息不足似乎使完整的视界无法实现。因此，亥姆霍兹在1867年创造了"无意识推论"这一术语，并提出视觉只能是某种"无意识推论"的结果。他提出大脑是根据已有的经验和不完整的数据来做出假设和结论。

我们不只"看到"这个世界，同时也创造了一个介于客观物理环境和个人体验及想象之间的世界。很多情况下我们并未意识到在表现客观真实世界的过程中所采用的主观视角。几个世纪以来，我们无意间在地图中应用着一种无形的知识编码，它以符合社会和文化习俗及传统技术的方式渲染着世界，或在不经意中推广特定的政治、社会和文化观点。

但艺术家们早就认识到这种现象，最近几十年，他们越来越为"地理学制图领域所蕴含的美与力量、真理与技巧、幻想与功能所着迷"（费迪南德，2019）。"地图艺术"已经成为艺术探索活动中的一个明确领域。在著作《超越度量：艺术、制图学和全球现代性空间》中，西蒙·费迪南德对该领域进行了深入探析。这本著作研究了各种基于地图的艺术作品，拓展了将地图视为对地理环境一成不变的表现这一传统观点。事实上，地图充满了主观的价值和视角，并引领我们超越固定的几何形态和空间量测。

表面之外

在现代科技的曙光中，人们发现了探索和可视化世界的新技术，使我们能够突破常见的事物表面。著名德国物理学家和机械工程师，维尔茨堡大学教授威廉·康拉德·伦琴于1895年发现了X射线，他于1901年被授予第一届诺贝尔物理学奖。基于该技术，高能量的电磁波可以穿过对于可见光来说不透明的材料。对人体而言，这

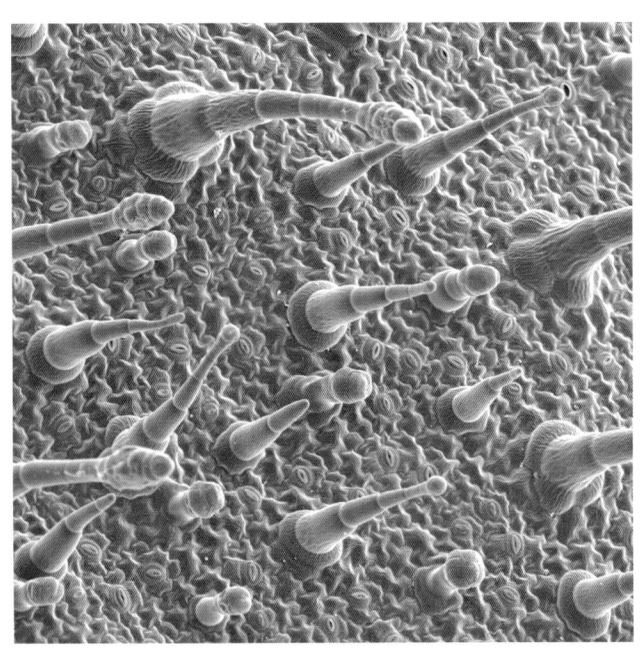

11 烟草上部叶片表面的扫描电子显微镜图像，可见毛状体和一些气孔. 制图: 路易莎·霍华德. 来源: 达特茅斯学院, 公共领域
Scanning electron microscope image of *Nicotiana alata* upper leaf surface, showing tricomes and a few stomates. Image by Louisa Howard. Source: Dartmouth College, public domain

12 木刻《白天和黑夜》，用灰色和黑色墨水印刷，莫里兹·柯尼利斯·埃舍尔作于1938年。来源：维基艺术百科
Day and Night, woodcut, printed in grey and black inks, made by M. C. Escher in 1938. Source: WikiArt

our conventional view that maps are an immutable arbiter of geographic fact. Imbued with subjective values and vision, they take us beyond the fixed geometry and measure of space.

Beyond the surface

At the dawn of the modern era, new techniques for probing and visualising the world were discovered. These new processes were able to let us see beyond the surface of the things we encounter in everyday life. Notably German physicist and mechanical engineer, a professor at Würzburg University, Wilhelm Conrad Röentgen discovered X-rays in 1895. He was awarded the first ever Noble Prize for Physics in 1901. In this process very high energy electromagnetic waves are fired through materials opaque to visible light. In the case of the human body, this enables the production of detailed ghost like images showing bones covered by flesh and muscle and normally invisible to sight. The interior of our bodies can now be revealed with extraordinary fidelity without recourse to damaging surgical procedures. The success of this work inspired a flood of new techniques and processes using other energy forms to probe beyond the surface. Today the use of sound, magnetic resonance and other pressure and electromagnetic waves has revolutionised how and what we can see.

One of the latest additions to the array of devices and techniques we have for recording and in turn representing the world we inhabit is the laser scanner. These instruments generate laser light and then project rapid pulses out into the world. When the laser pulse encounters a physical surface it is reflected back to the scanner. The scanner detects the returning laser pulse, and by calculating the time interval between sending the pulse and sensing the return, it is able to calculate the distance to the object. The scanner precisely records distance and orientation. The latest scanning equipment emits from hundreds of thousands to millions of pulses a second. It moves in a precise and calibrated sequence to cast its eye across the full surrounding environment. The position of each of the millions of recorded points in space can then be placed in a computer program to create a 'point cloud', a dimensionally accurate virtual 3D model of the place scanned. Many scanners simultaneously take a 360° panoramic photo of the environment and are able to assign a colour to each point in space.

A similar outcome can be achieved through the processes of photogrammetry. Computer programs and software can analyse the attributes of what can be thousands of photos by capturing the same object or environment from multiple angles and locations. The program is able to calculate three dimensional form from this data and again construct a virtual three dimensional model. Unlike X-rays or ultrasound techniques, laser scanning and photogrammetry cannot probe beyond the visible. Howev-

种技术可以产生鬼魅般的精细图像，用来显示通常不可见的肌肉和被肌肉覆盖的骨骼，从而我们不必借助破坏性的外科手术就可以真切地观察到身体的内部情况。这激发了使用其他能量形式探测表面之外世界的大量新技术和新工艺，声音、磁共振以及其他压力和电磁波的使用已经彻底改变了我们的观察方式和内容。

激光扫描仪是我们用于记录和再现外部环境的新设备之一。它能产生激光，然后将高速脉冲投射到空间中。当激光脉冲遇到物理表面时，它将反射回扫描仪。扫描仪检测返回的激光脉冲，并通过计算脉冲往返的时间推导物体的距离。该设备能准确记录距离和方向。最新的扫描设备每秒发出数十万至数百万个脉冲，它以精确且经过校准的顺序移动，将射线投向整个周围环境，然后可以将数百万个记录点中的每个点的位置导入计算机程序，以创建"点云"，即某个扫描位置尺寸精确的虚拟三维模型。许多扫描仪可以同时拍摄360°全景环境照片，并可以给空间中的每个点着色。

摄影测量也可以实现类似的目的：计算机程序和软件可以分析从多个角度和多个位置捕获同一对象或环境的大量照片的属性，并能从该数据中计算出三维空间信息和构建虚拟模型。与X射线或超声技术不同，激光扫描和摄影测量无法探测不可见物体，但这些技术创造出的三维模型展现出一种发展前景，为人们提供了在现实环境中无法获取的视角。目前我们还在探索虚拟现实并尝试去更多地了解和更好地操控这项技术，这为我们建立观察和理解世界的新视角提供了重要机遇。

作为该方向的重要技术之一，虚拟现实（VR）提供了新的空间和感官体验，并具有诱人的前景。理论上讲，沉浸式虚拟现实可以无缝模拟和增强真实世界中的体验。头戴式装备和其他假肢设备将我们带入一个与现实世界融为一体的网络环境，当我们在VR中移动时，世界的变化方式与我们在物理环境中的感受几乎相同。除了视觉之外，物理环境的听觉模拟也可以构成体验的一部分。未来的挑战是引入全感官互动，研究人员、发明家、创意人员、设计师、工程师等正在积极探索，我们很难预测未来，也许与真实体验毫无差别的虚拟环境会更早到来。

13 拙政园的虚拟现实体验，其中园林的虚拟模型为跨越历史的旅行提供了场景
Virtual reality experience at Zhuozheng Garden (Humble Administrator Garden). A virtual model of the garden provides the setting for a journey through history

14 上海豫园三维点云扫描模型
The 3D point cloud scanning model of Yuyuan Garden in Shanghai

er the capacity to create three dimensional models that can be controlled and transformed in cyberspace offers the prospect of projections and ways of seeing not available to someone in the physical world. Virtual models can be manipulated in ways that we are just beginning to discover and understand to present us with new views and understandings of the world.

Virtual reality (VR) is one such direction. It offers the tantalising promise of new spatial and sensory experience. In the immersive world of VR, our lived experience is, at least in theory, seamlessly simulated and perhaps extended. Headsets and other prosthetic devices transport us into cyber environments that we cannot distinguish from the physical world of daily life. As we move in VR, the world changes in the same way that we perceive movement through the physical world. In addition to the visual, auditory simulations of physical environments can form part of the experience. The next challenge is to incorporate a full sensory engagement. Already the army of researchers, inventors, creatives, designers, engineers and others has enthusiastically taken on this task, and in the near future who knows what advances we will witness. That promise of a virtual experience indistinguishable from the experience of the physical world is perhaps closer than many might imagine.

何园

2018—2019年，笔者多次考察何园，并测绘这一重要园林遗产。其中的关键工作是使用Leica BLK360激光扫描仪完成三维扫描。这些扫描成果已合并为一个数据集并生成整个园林的虚拟模型。这个虚拟点云模型是何园文化遗产的一个高精度记录，并形成一项永久的档案。本书采用了一系列独特而广泛的再现手段，包括点云正射影像平面图、立面图、剖面图，以及关于园林不同部分的多视角渲染图。尽管以前的许多出版物都提供了关于何园的测绘图及相关材料，但并未能提供类似的详细记录和精确数据。同时，本书的图纸创新性地结合了测绘科学和园林艺术的视角，从而对历史园林展开全面记录和再现。本书采用了正交投影图形式，同时借助高度风格化的图像，尝试超越主观和客观的界限，并赋予各种视角同等的价值。毫无疑问，本书内容的构思还包含着笔者对当代文化价值观的思考和见解。

我们希望探索的是一种新的、客观但又令人回味的古典园林遗产记录方式。书中的图纸以等比例几何投影图为主，但它们亦可以唤起人们对园林遗产中活动、生命、光影、形态和纹理的多样化感受。因此，这些图纸并不是纯粹的复制，更不是一种对物理世界完全的还原。这些二维印刷图像的最终效果也受到书籍生产技术和过程影响。本书尝试提供一种新的样式，以一种新的方式学习和理解园林遗产，同时也希望提供一个新的视角来捕捉和表达场所的意境和氛围，重新唤起人们的记忆。

Heyuan Garden

In 2018 and 2019, the authors visited Heyuan Garden on a number of separate occasions to survey and document the site. One of the key activities was to complete an extensive series of 3D scans using a Leica BLK360 laser scanner. These scans have been combined into a single data set creating a virtual model of the whole site. The combined point cloud model provides a detailed and dimensionally accurate survey of the garden precinct and can become an enduring archival record. This publication presents a unique and extensive scaled series of photo realistic orthographic plans, elevations, sections and views of the garden and its various elements. While numerous previous publications have presented survey documents and material from the garden, none have been able to accomplish outcomes with the level of detail and dimensional accuracy presented in this document and accompanying data sets. But more than this, the graphic representations included here present the garden both with a scientific level of rigour and authority, and the subjective perspective of the artist. They employ the conventions and certainty of orthographic projection while at the same time offering a highly stylised and edited set of images. These representations aim to transcend the subjective/objective divide recognising and placing equal value in each point of view. They also undoubtedly have embedded a set of contemporary cultural values implicit in who we are and our place in the world.

What we have aimed to achieve is an objective but evocative record and representation of the garden; illustrations and views that are primarily scaled geometric projections but that evoke movement and life, light and shade, form and texture. There is no sense here that this is some untainted copy and document that is a facsimile of the physical world. These are two dimensional printed images that rely on the techniques and processes available for the production of a book; but that attempt to provide a reference point for extending understanding and study while offering a new visual perspective capturing the mood and feel of place or rekindling the memory of a visit.

04 数字化园林遗产图录计划
Garden Heritage Digital Document Project

为何记录中国古典园林遗产？

人是一种天生健忘的动物，离开物质性的记录，我们可能连数月前发生的事都很难记清。对于文化遗产来说，记录则更加重要。人文地理学家段义孚先生在其著作《经验透视中的空间与地方》（1977）中提到："一座城市并不会只因为其长时间存在而成为历史城市。历史上的事件如果不被历史书、纪念物、表演，以及持续不断的传统节庆活动所纪念，就不会对今天产生影响。"因此，记录首先是为了传承记忆，我们需要通过记录来保存文化遗产所蕴含的历史信息，延续文化遗产的价值。2019年4月15日，法国巴黎圣母院的火灾再一次提醒我们文化遗产记录的重要性。比利时艺术史学家安德鲁·塔隆先生在2015年采集的高精度三维激光扫描数据成为巴黎圣母院灾后重建最为重要的依据之一。当文化遗产的本体遭到破坏，记录将是我们接触遗产信息唯一的途径。因此，遗产记录的重要性完全可以和遗产的物质本体相提并论。早在1996年，国际古迹遗址理事会（ICOMOS）就颁布了《记录古迹、建筑组群和遗址的准则》，指出"记录遗产是遗产地相关责任组织和个人的必要义务，也是保护过程的核心组成部分"。

除了保存遗产信息之外，记录还有更加广泛而深刻的意义。从遗产研究出发，记录是理解遗产价值最为有效的途径之一。在开展记录的过程中，首先需要对遗产的产生和发展过程进行深入探究，这将自然而然地增进我们对相关历史的认知，并加深对文化、价值、身份等重要问题的理解。从遗产实践出发，记录是遗产保护和管理的重要信息基础。充分的遗产档案是修复、维护和解说等工作的必要依据，更是监测遗产变化的科学参照，这对于恒变中的园林类遗产来说尤为重要。我们需要确保园林的日常维护对于其历史特征和文化价值具有高度的敏感性，并将园林的变化控制在可接受的范围内，而这

Why do we need to record the heritage of Chinese classical gardens?

Humans are naturally forgetful creatures. Without material records we may not be able to remember what happened a few months ago. For cultural heritage, the record is even more important. The human geographer Yi-Fu Tuan mentioned in his book *Space and Place: The Perspective of Experience* (1977): 'a city does not become a historic city merely because it has occupied the same site for a long time. Past events make no impact on the present unless they are memorialised in history books, monuments, pageants, and solemn and jovial festivities that are recognised as part of an ongoing tradition.' Therefore, the primary purpose of recording is to inherit the memory. We need to preserve the memory contained in the cultural heritage through records, and continue the culture and value of the heritage. The fire of Notre Dame de Paris, France, on 15 April, 2019, once again alerted us to the importance of our cultural heritage record. The high-precision 3D laser scanning data collected by a Belgian art historian Andrew Tallon in 2015 has become one of the most important foundations for the reconstruction of Notre Dame. When the physical evidence of cultural heritage is destroyed, the record will be the only way we can access the heritage information. Therefore, the importance of the record can be compared with the material ontology of the heritage. As early as 1996, the International Council on Monuments and Sites (ICOMOS) promulgated the *Principles for the Recording of Monuments, Groups of Buildings and Sites*, stating that 'recording heritage is a necessary obligation of the responsible organizations and individuals involved in the site and is also the core of the conservation process'.

In addition to preserving cultural heritage information, records have a broader and deeper meaning. Recording is an effective approach to understand the value of heritage. In the process of carrying out the record, we first need to conduct in-depth exploration of the process of the birth and development of cultural heritage, which will naturally enhance our understanding of history, and thus deepen our understanding of important issues such as culture, value and identity. From the perspective of protection practice, the heritage record is an important information basis for heritage conservation and management. A good cultural heritage archive is a necessary basis for repair, maintenance and interpretation, and it is a scientific reference for monitoring changes in heritage. This is especially important for the ever-changing cultural heritage of gardens. We need to ensure that daily maintenance is highly sensitive to the historical and cultural values of the garden and that the changes in the garden are controlled to an acceptable level. All need comprehensive and scientific record data as a support. In addition, records are an important medium for promoting public understanding and appreciation of cultural heritage. With the help of sound representation and interpretation, the public can more intuitively accept the information of the heritage and appreciate the value of the heritage. The profound historical information and difficult technical terms can be presented through simple and easy-to-understand drawings, to enhance people's interest in the heritage protection. In short, cultural heritage protection is an ongoing process, and heritage record information is an important basis for this process. Without continuous collection and sharing of heritage information, heritage protection becomes a source of waterlessness. Therefore, the scientific record of cultural heritage is an important task

15 无锡寄畅园,2018年4月,彩色照片是记录古典园林最直接、最常用的方式之一
Jichang Garden (Solace-Imbued Garden) in Wuxi, China, April 2018, colour photographs are one of the most direct and common ways to record classical gardens

that must be carried out continuously by different groups, different eras and different regions.

The Chinese classical garden is the combined work of nature and humans. It is a typical 'clearly defined landscape', reflecting the unique aesthetic of 'naturally, above nature' in Chinese classical culture and the artistic pursuit of ancient Chinese cultural elites. Chinese classical gardens are profound and long-standing. They have been continuously improved during the development of more than two thousand years, forming a complete planning, design, construction and even system of aesthetics. They have also influenced gardening practices in Asia, Europe, and countries and regions of other continents and achieved a unique position in the history of gardens in the world. In China, a large number of classical gardens are still preserved. They are the precious evidence of the brilliant achievements of ancient Chinese landscape civilisation, and they are an important part of the treasure of all human culture and art. Therefore, the scientific and comprehensive record of the heritage of Chinese classical gardens is self-evident.

Due to various reasons, the records of classical gardens in Chinese history are mostly written, and there are few drawings. Many garden drawings pay more attention to artistic expression and ignore the imitation of specific forms, which brings difficulties to us to intuitively understand and study Chinese classical gardens today. From the perspective of protecting garden heritage, the systematic investigation and recording of classical garden heritage by modern surveying and mapping began in China in the 1930s. The famous garden experts, such as Liu Dunzhen, Tong Jun and Chen Congzhou, conducted systematic investigation and mapping of classical garden remains, leaving many maps and records, which not only provided important information for later classical garden research and restoration, but also became important historical documents. Since the founding of People's Republic of China, with the strengthening of the concept of cultural relics protection, the National Cultural Relics Department has gradually begun to do filed investigation on the ancient garden heritage, and established systematic garden records and archives. At the same time, colleges and universities with architecture and landscape architecture in China have opened courses related to ancient gardens, and organised surveying and mapping internships according to the academic tradition of architectural education. The survey covers most of the country and has formed more and more achievements. A large number of surveys have accumulated a wealth of information. Many classical gardens have been recorded and used in related research and protection practices, which played an important role in promoting the modern conservation of China's classical garden heritage.

However, if we re-examine the records of Chinese classical gardens from the perspective of contemporary cultural heritage conservation, we will find that the current results have certain limitations. First is the accuracy of the recorded data. Limited by traditional measuring methods with tape measure, theodolite and level gauge as the main tools, the integrity and accuracy of ancient garden surveying data are insufficient, especially for irregular components such as pools, rockeries and terrain. The previous main method to measure key points is flawed and it is impossible to accurately measure and depict more complex garden spatial information. For example, in the existing garden drawings,

一切都需要全面、科学的记录数据作为支撑。从文化信息传播的角度来看，记录是促进公众理解并欣赏文化遗产的重要媒介。借助语音导览和解说，公众可以更加直接地接收遗产信息，进而珍视遗产价值。复杂的遗产特征和难懂的专业术语可以通过简洁易懂的图纸呈现，以增强人们对遗产保护的兴趣。遗产保护是一项长期持续的工作，而调查和记录是这项工作的起点和重要的基础，缺少了不断采集、整理和分享遗产信息的过程，遗产保护也就成了无源之水。因此，科学记录文化遗产是不同群体、不同时代、不同地域都必须持续开展的重要工作。

中国古典园林是人与自然共同的杰作，是典型的"有意设计的文化景观"，反映了中国古典文化中"本于自然、高于自然"的独特景观审美和中国古代文化精英的崇高艺术追求。中国古典园林博大精深、源远流长，在其两千余年的发展演进过程中不断完善，形成了完整的规划、设计、建造乃至艺术审美体系，并对亚洲、欧洲和世界其他大洲的国家、地区的园林产生重要影响，在世界园林史上拥有独特的地位。目前在中国仍保存着大量的古典园林作品，它们是古代景观文明辉煌成就的珍贵证据，更是全人类文化艺术宝库的重要组成部分。因此，对中国古典园林遗产进行科学、全面的记录，其意义不言而喻。

由于种种原因，历史上对于中国古典园林的记录以文字居多，较少有图纸保存。很多园林图画更加注重意境表达而不强调对具体形态的精确模仿，这给我们了解和研究历史上出现过的园林带来了困难。从保护园林遗产的角度而言，用现代测绘的方法对中国古典园林遗产进行系统的考察和记录始于20世纪30年代。刘敦桢、童寯、陈从周等老一代古建园林专家对古典园林遗存进行了系统的调查和测绘，留下了不少测绘图纸，不仅为后来的园林研究和修复提供了重要资料，也对园林历史档案的建立有很大助益。中华人民共和国成立以来，随着文物保护理念的加强，国家文物部门逐渐开始对古典园林遗产进行调查统计，建立了系统的园林记录和档案。同时，中国设有建筑和园林专业的院校均开设了古建园林的相关课程，并按照学院派建筑教育传统组织测绘实习，其范围覆盖全国大部分地区，形成了越来越多的成果。大量实测调查积累了丰富的资料，许多现存的古典园林得到了记录，并用于相关研究和保护实践之中，为推动我国古典园林遗产的现代化保护起到了重要的作用。

然而，若以当代文化遗产保护的视角重新审视对中国古典园林的记录，会发现目前的成果有一定的局限性。其一在于记录数据的准确性：受限于以卷尺、经纬仪、水准仪为主要工具的传统测量手段，古典园林测绘数据的精确性存在不足，尤其是水池、假山、地形等不规则要素的测绘数据，过去以测量关键点为主的方法存在缺陷，无法精确测量和描绘较为复杂的不规则园林环境。例如，现有园林图纸中对园林假山空间的测绘大多数为示意性绘图，较好者对山体平面轮廓和竖向层次有概括性的模拟，较差者甚至寥寥几笔仅作示意性表达。更为普遍的是，同一园林的不同版本平面图常常在池山形态方面存在较大的差异，导致相关研究和保护工作缺少科学的依据。其二在于测绘数据的完整性：虽然中国古典园林调查记录工作已经开展了几十年，但仍有大量古典园林遗存并未得到完整的记录。许多调查测绘是以分析造园手法为目标，这部分记录虽然能够反映园林的空间特征和营构法则，但对于保护和监测来说，数据不够完善准确，标准化程度亦有所欠缺，且仍然带有过多的主观成分。其三，古典园林记录的时效性也是重要问题：园林是动态变化的遗产，山池花木随时间而变，建筑设施也不断更新，就算是与20世纪初相比，大量古典园林已经历了多次修复和改造，早期的记录往往不能反映

most of the surveying and mapping of the garden rockery space is a schematic drawing. The better ones have a general simulation of the contour and the vertical level of the mountain, and the poor ones even only contain a few lines just to symbolise the location and scope of the mountain. More generally, different versions of the same garden often have large differences in the shape of ponds and rockeries, resulting in a lack of scientific basis for relevant research and conservation work. Second is the integrity of the survey data. Although the investigation and recording of Chinese classical gardens has been carried out for several decades, there are still many classical gardens remaining that have not been fully recorded. Most of the surveying and mapping is aimed at analysing the garden design. While this part of the record can reflect the characteristics and construction rules of the gardens, it still carries many subjective elements and lacks the precision and standardisation for protection and monitoring. Third, the timeliness of classical garden records is also an important issue. The garden is a kind of dynamic and changing heritage. The mountains and flowers change with time, and the building facilities are constantly updated. Even compared with the early 20th century, many classical gardens have undergone many changes, and the existing records often cannot reflect the reality of the garden. The situation cannot provide strong support for the conservation and management of heritage. However, traditional surveying and mapping methods are often time-consuming and labor-intensive, ranging from a few weeks to many months. It takes a lot of time to completely map an ancient garden, and it is almost impossible to update the survey data regularly. Fourth, the dissemination of the heritage record has not been fully reflected in current conservation practices. The traditional line orthographic projection in the architecture discipline has been used as the main method of recording, which is too professional to be understood by the public. Paper archives are often preserved by the protection and management departments, which are difficult for the public to obtain. The way in which classical garden heritage information is expressed and shared is also urgently needed to be updated. In summary, the recording and protection of contemporary Chinese classical garden heritage requires new ideas, new methods and new technologies.

Opportunities and challenges brought about by digitalisation

From a technical point of view, digitisation is to transform many complex and variable information into measurable numbers and data, and then use these numbers and data to establish appropriate digital models, transform them into a series of binary codes, and introduce them into computers for unified processing. Nicholas Negroponte said in his book *Digital Being*: 'Computation is no longer only about computers, it determines our survival.' For the conservation of cultural heritage, the impact of digital technology is also revolutionary. The rapid development and maturity of digital technology provides an unprecedented opportunity for us to understand and analyse complex heritage objects, and will also subvert the current methods of information collection, processing, management and dissemination for cultural heritage. This subversion will first be reflected in the cultural heritage record. The collection of heritage information no longer depends on traditional tools. The new digital mapping technology represented by the three technologies i.e. drone, laser scanning and close-range photogrammetry is gradually replacing manual survey

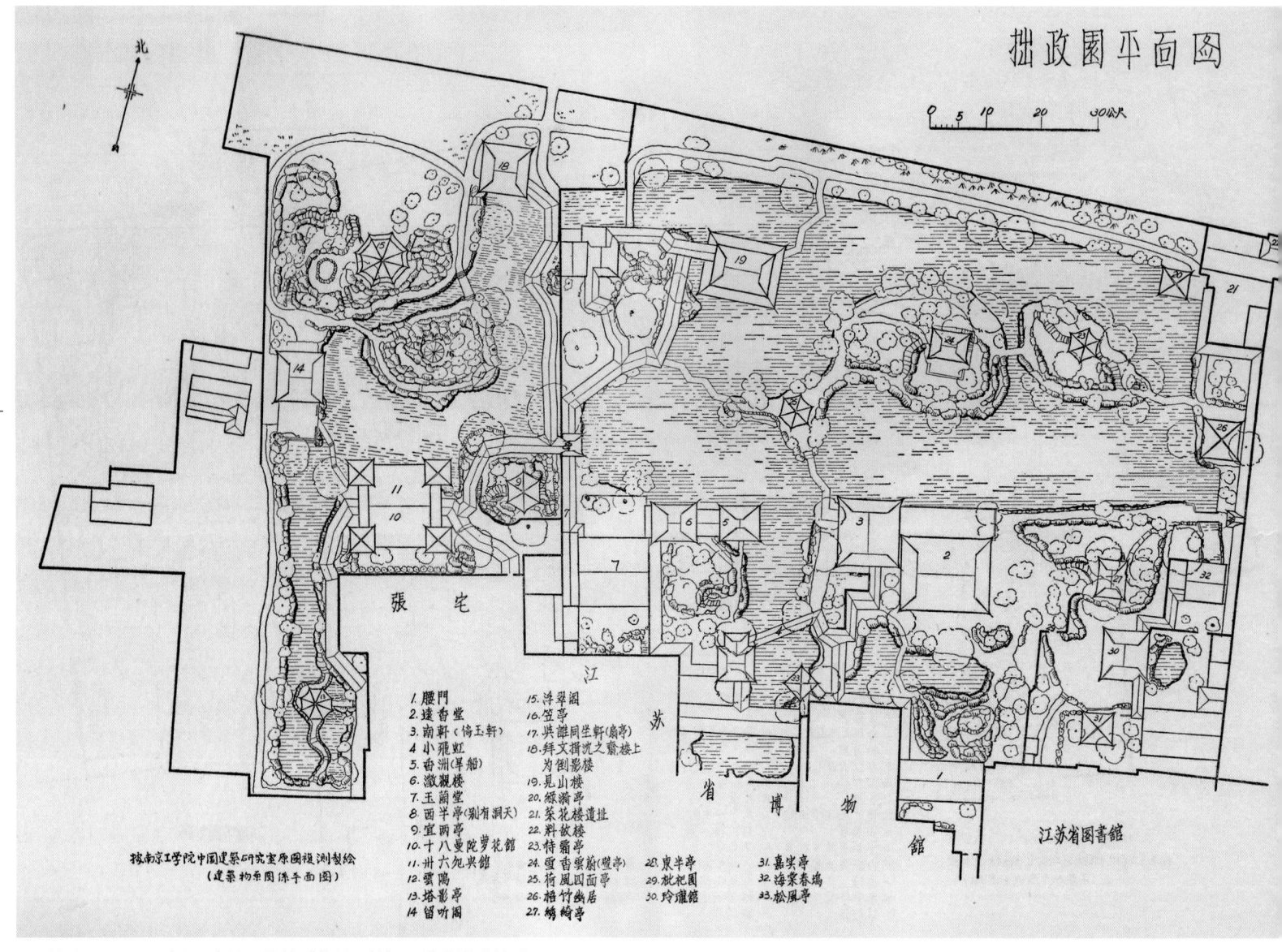

16 拙政园平面图. 来源：陈从周编著，《苏州园林》，同济大学建筑系，同济大学教材科，1956年

Plan of Zhuozheng Garden (Humble Administrator Garden).
Source: Chen Congzhou eds, *Suzhou Gardens*, Department of Architecture, Tongji University, 1956

and drawing, and becoming the main means of obtaining information on cultural heritage space. New technologies are revolutionary in terms of coverage, integrity and accuracy. The spatial data acquisition by new surveying and mapping technologies is fast and efficient. The high-precision heritage space information can be obtained without many ground controls points. At the same time, laser scanning and multi-spectral photography can be used to layer the ground reflection information and automatically distinguish different heritage garden components and attributes. The new mapping technology also provides 3D spatial data in centimetres or even millimetres of precision, and produces high quality digital elevation models. Light Detection and Ranging (LiDAR) tools can penetrate the vegetation in the landscape and obtain surface elevation information. More importantly, the new mapping technology does not need to touch the target object during the collection process, which is very important for the more vulnerable targets such as ancient trees and buildings. It must be noted that the new mapping technology has a short operating cycle and is easy to update, so the timeliness of the data is strong, which will enable dynamic monitoring of cultural heritage. The advancement and innovation of digital technology has provided an unprecedented opportunity for the recording and protection of Chinese classical gardens. Many limitations of the traditional surveying and mapping mentioned above will make breakthroughs with the advancement of technology.

At present, two-dimensional line graphics with real-life photos are still the main means of the expression and dissemination of cultural heritage information. The two-dimensional line graphic mainly depicts the spatial information such as size, proportion and structure of the heritage. The photos reflect the attribute information of the heritage environment, including colour, material and style. But in coming years, the development and maturity of 3D point cloud technology will likely change this approach. A point cloud is a collection of points that express the spatial distribution and surface characteristics of a target under the same spatial reference system. Each point contains the three-dimensional coordinate information of the object and the attribute information such as colour and material. Through the 3D point cloud model, both the spatial and attribute information of the heritage site can be visually and simultaneously expressed. Using laser scanning or digital photogrammetry devices, we can capture high-quality 3D point cloud data and simulate and visualise the spatial form of the heritage with unprecedented precision. By reading the three-dimensional space information and constructing the model by computer, it is extremely easy to view and analyse the colour and material of the heritage in the virtual environment. Virtual simulation software can be used to observe, cut, and render the surface of each part of the cultural heritage. It is also possible to measure the scale of any detail in the model. We can render the point cloud model in pixels and generate high-resolution projections to obtain model isometric, perspective or orthodograph images. Compared with the two-dimensional line graphic, the point cloud model can better reflect the material details of the heritage object and improve the heritage file. If necessary, we can also easily extract two-dimensional line graphics of different surfaces from point cloud images. With the maturity of point cloud technology and the reduction of cost in recent years, point cloud technology has been increasingly used in the recording, expression and protection of cultural heritage. It can also combine the line graphics and real-life photos in the traditional her-

园林的现实情况，无法为遗产保护和管理提供有力支撑。传统测绘方法往往耗时费力，完整地测绘一座古园林需要大量时间，少则数周，多则数月，几乎不可能做到及时的数据更新。其四，园林遗产记录的价值还未充分体现：以线划平面图为主的传统记录方式专业性强，公众较难完全理解；纸质档案往往被保护和管理部门保存，公众难以获取，古典园林遗产信息表达和共享的方式也亟待更新。综上所述，当代中国古典园林遗产的记录和保护需要新思路、新方法和新技术。

数字化带来的机遇和挑战

所谓数字化，就是将许多复杂多变的信息转变为可以度量的数字和数据，再以这些数字、数据建立适当的数字化模型，把它们转变为一系列二进制代码，在计算机内部进行统一处理。尼古拉·尼葛洛庞帝在其著作《数字化生存》中开篇就谈到："计算不再只和计算机有关，它决定我们的生存。"对于文化遗产保护来说，数字化技术所带来的冲击同样是革命性的，数字技术的快速发展和成熟为我们了解和分析复杂的遗产对象提供了前所未有的机会，同时也将颠覆目前文化遗产信息采集、处理、管理和传播的方法。这种颠覆性首先将体现在文化遗产记录方面，遗产信息的采集不再只依赖传统工具，以无人机、激光雷达和近景摄影测量三大技术为代表的新型数字化测绘技术正在逐渐取代人工测绘而成为获取文化遗产空间信息的主要手段。新技术无论在覆盖度、完整性和精确性等层面，其提升都是革命性的。新型测绘技术采集空间数据速度快、效率高，无需大量地面控制点就可以获得高精度的遗产空间信息。同时，利用激光雷达或多光谱摄影等技术可以对地物反射信息进行分层，自动区别不同的遗产园林要素和属性。新型测绘技术还可以提供厘米甚至毫米精度的三维空间数据并生成高质量的数字高程模型。借助激光雷达可以穿透景观中的植被，并获取地表高程信息。更为重要的是，新型测绘技术在采集过程中不需要接触被测目标物，这对园林中的古树名木、古建筑等较为脆弱的目标物有重要意义。必须要说明的是，新型测绘技术作业周期短，易于更新，因此数据的时效性强，这将使文化遗产的动态监测成为可能。数字技术的进步和革新为中国古典园林的记录和保护提供了不可估量的机遇，前文提到的传统园林测绘存在的诸多局限，都将随着技术的全面应用获得突破性进展。

目前，二维线划图配以实景照片仍旧是文化遗产记录的主要方式。二维线划图主要表达的是遗产的尺寸、比例、结构等空间信息，实景照片则反映的是遗产的外部环境所包含的色彩、材质和样式等属性信息。但近年来，三维点云技术的发展和成熟将有可能改变这种方式。点云是指在同一空间参考系下表达目标空间分布和表面特性的海量点的集合，每个点包含目标对象的三维空间坐标信息以及色彩、材质等属性信息。通过三维点云模型可以同时直观地表达遗产的空间和属性两类信息。利用激光雷达或数码影像能够获取高质量的三维点云数据，并以前所未有的精度对遗产的空间形态进行模拟和可视化。通过计算机读取三维空间信息并进行模型构建，能够极为简便地在虚拟环境中观赏和分析遗产的色彩、材质等特征。利用虚拟仿真软件能够任意观察、剖切、渲染文化遗产的各部分表面，还可以在模型中测量任何细节的尺度。我们可以以像素方式对点云模型进行渲染并生成高分辨率影像，获得模型轴测图、透视图或者正射影像图等。与二维线划图相比，点云模型能够更好地反映遗产对象的材质细节，使遗产档案获得质的提升。如果有需要，我们也能十分便捷地从点云影像中提取不同表面的二维线划图。随着软硬件的成熟以及成本的降低，点云技术已经越来越多地应用于文化遗产的记录、展示和保护，它可以融合并同时传递线划图和实景照片所包含的信息，极大地提升记录质量，并有可能改变未来遗产信息传播的方式。

itage recording methods. The function of the results greatly improves the quality of the results and will most likely change the way in which the information is transmitted.

In France, photographs quickly replaced the mainstream miniature portrait painting and reproductive engraving techniques in the 19th century, making it the first choice for recording characters and the external environment. This technological innovation has had an important impact on European heritage conservation concepts. Photos capture the details of objects with unprecedented precision, allowing changes in heritage to be recorded and portrayed. This led people to gradually examine the changes in heritage from a scientific perspective and expand to the understanding and discussion of authenticity. At the same time, due to the wide application of photographs, the original is no longer the only source of heritage information. It can also provide a heritage experience through photographs. At the time, this technological innovation led to the emergence of new museums for educational purposes and a museum turned out to be a platform to disseminate cultural information, rather than just a place to collect cultural relics. Today, the rapid development and maturity of digital technology has made it easier than ever to acquire high-precision three-dimensional spatial information, providing us with new opportunities to recognise cultural heritage and promote the development of conservation concepts. Heritage information will also be increasingly transmitted in the form of 'bits' through computers and the Internet, and digital records are becoming an important medium for inheriting the value of heritage. Technological innovation will also promote the development of cultural heritage conservation concepts.

2020 will be the first year that 5G mobile communication technology enters commercial use, which may bring about the seventh information revolution in human society. In the future of cultural heritage conservation, we are likely to witness some changes and may face some challenges. Firstly, it will be very convenient to obtain high-precision spatial information. Compared with today, the cost of heritage data collection will be greatly reduced. The main way of recording and expressing cultural heritage is no longer a two-dimensional line graphic, but a digital three-dimensional model. The ensuing question is how to set relevant standards and specifications for digital three-dimensional heritage files to make them more widely used and disseminated. Secondly, the advancement of digital technology has made it possible to dynamically monitor the cultural heritage of gardens, thus realising the scientific conservation and monitoring of cultural heritage, which will greatly increase the demand for three-dimensional archives of cultural heritage. As a result, the demand and requirements for digital heritage professionals in cultural heritage will increase significantly. At the same time, with the maturity of virtual reality technology, the virtual reality experience of the cultural heritage will greatly enhance the simulation and restoration of real scenes, and many virtual experiences will appear. The problem with this advancement is how to evaluate and manage the cultural heritage virtual environment. The cultural heritage management department not only has to manage the physical space, but also needs to supervise the virtual space. From the above, therefore, the digital heritage protection theory will be a new field of contemporary cultural heritage research.

19世纪的法国，摄影技术的出现使得照片很快取代了当时主流的微缩画像技术和手工可复制版画技术，成为对人物和外部环境进行记录的第一选择。这一技术革新曾给欧洲的遗产保护理念带来重要影响。照片能够以更高的精度捕捉对象的细节，使得遗产的变化可以被记录和描绘。这使得人们逐渐以科学的眼光审视遗产的变化，并拓展到对于真实性的关注和讨论。由于照片的广泛应用，原物不再是遗产信息的唯一来源，通过照片同样可以为人们提供遗产体验。当时这种技术的革新促使了以教育为目的的新型博物馆的出现，博物馆不再是只是收藏文物的场所，而更多作为传播文化信息的平台。今天，数字技术的迅速发展和成熟使得获取高精度三维空间信息变得非常便捷，为我们重新认知文化遗产并推动保护理念的发展提供了新的机遇。遗产信息也会越来越多地通过计算机和互联网以"比特"的形式传播，数字化记录开始转变为传承遗产价值的重要媒介，技术的革新也必将推动文化遗产保护理念的发展。

2020年将是5G移动通信技术进入商用的第一年，这很可能带来人类历史上的第七次信息革命。在未来的文化遗产保护中，我们很可能见证一些变化，也可能面临一些挑战。首先，获取高精度空间信息将变得非常便捷，与今天相比，遗产数据采集的成本也会大大降低，文化遗产记录和表现的主要方式不再是二维线划图，而是数字化三维模型。随之而来的问题是如何为数字化三维遗产档案设定相关的标准和规范，使之更加广泛地应用和传播。其次，数字技术的进步使得园林类文化遗产的动态监测成为可能，从而真正实现文化遗产的科学保护和监测，这将大大增加文化遗产三维档案的建档需求。因此，对于文化遗产数字技术专业人员的需求和要求也将随之增长和有所提升。同时随着虚拟现实技术的日益成熟，文化遗产虚拟体验对现实场景的模拟还原能力将会大大增强，大量虚拟体验将会出现。这种进步带来的问题是如何对文化遗产虚拟环境进行评估和管理。文化遗产管理部门不仅要管理物理空间，也需要对虚拟空间进行监管。因此，"数字遗产保护理论"将是当代文化遗产研究的新领域。

数字化园林遗产图录计划

基于中国古典园林所面临的现实问题和新技术带来的机遇，我们于2018年启动了数字化园林遗产图录（GHDD）计划，运用前沿数字技术探索中国古典园林遗产记录和保护的新途径。该计划由国际古迹遗址理事会－国际风景园林师联合会文化景观科学委员会数字化文化景观研究工作小组领衔，受同济大学建筑与城市规划学院一流团队科研基金、同济大学建筑与城市规划学院建成环境技术中心共同资助，并先后受到同济大学测绘与地理信息学院、澳大利亚格里菲斯大学建筑系、联合国教科文组织亚太地区世界遗产培训与研究中心等一系列高校、组织和单位的支持和协助。GHDD计划将选取10处具有代表性的中国古典园林遗产，采用国际文化遗产档案框架和标准，利用新型数字技术建立高质量遗产图录，弥补现有古典园林记录资料的不足。我们希望能够为中国古典园林遗产提供一种可以持续开展的数字化记录手段，并将其推广到高校、科研院所和园林管理部门，使得园林遗产的现代化研究、管理和监测成为可能。GHDD计划将全面探索中国古典园林数字化档案的基本思路和内容，包括园林遗产测绘形式、绘图方式和表现手法，更全面、完整、科学地展现中国古典园林的特征和价值。同时，我们也希望通过GHDD计划搭建数据交流平台，使得公众可以便捷地获得高质量的文化遗产数据，拉近文化遗产与专家、公众、管理者和学生之间的距离，推动遗产研究和保护理念的进步。

Garden Heritage Digital Document project

Based on the problems faced by Chinese classical gardens and the opportunities brought by new technologies, we established the Garden Heritage Digital Document (GHDD) project in 2018, using cutting-edge digital technology to explore new ways of recording and protecting Chinese classical gardens. The project is led by the ICOMOS-IFLA International Scientific Committee on Cultural Landscapes (ISCCL), the Digital Culture Landscape Research Working Group, and subsidised by the innovative team research fund of the College of Architecture and Urban Planning at Tongji University, and the Built Environment Technology Center in the College of Architecture and Urban Planning in Tongji University. The project has been supported by and included participation from a series of universities and organisations, such as the School of Surveying and Geoinformatics of Tongji University, the Department of Architecture of Griffith University of Australia, and the World Heritage Institute of Training and Research for the Asia and the Pacific Region (Shanghai) under the auspices of UNESCO. The GHDD project plans to select ten representative cases of Chinese classical gardens, adopt international cultural heritage archive frameworks and standards, and use new digital technologies to establish high-quality heritage archives to make up for the shortcomings of existing classical garden records. It is hoped that it can provide a continuous digital recording method for Chinese classical garden heritage. This method can be quickly extended to universities, research institutes and garden management departments, making research, management and monitoring of garden heritage modernisation possible. The GHDD project will comprehensively explore the basic ideas and contents of the digital documents of Chinese classical gardens, including the means of mapping and drawing of garden heritage, drawing methods and means of representation, and more comprehensive, complete and scientific representation of the characteristics and values of Chinese classical gardens. At the same time, we also hope to build a data exchange platform through the GHDD project, so that the public can easily obtain high-quality cultural heritage data, thus shortening the distance between cultural heritage and experts, the public, managers and students, and promoting the improvement of heritage conservation concepts.

As the first Chinese classical garden for GHDD project, Heyuan Garden provided excellent conditions for exploring the digital documentation of Chinese classical gardens. First, Heyuan Garden is known as the 'First Garden of the Late Qing Dynasty'. It is the last work of Yangzhou's large-scale garden in the late feudal society. It is also the largest existing private garden in Yangzhou. It inherits the essence of Chinese traditional garden art and has a very high typicality and representativeness among Chinese classical private gardens. Second, the garden is large in scale, including all the elements of Chinese classical gardens, and has some unique features in garden rockery and architectural design. These elements and features are valuable materials to test new digital mapping technologies. Third, Yangzhou's local garden history research has a relatively deep accumulation, which has established a good theoretical support for our surveying and mapping. Finally, Heyuan Garden has a sound management system, a relatively good protection status and the appropriate conditions for digital mapping work. We established the plan for surveying and mapping

作为GHDD计划测绘的第一座中国古典园林，何园为探索中国古典园林数字化记录提供了良好的条件。何园被称作"晚清第一园"，是中国封建社会晚期扬州大型园林的最后作品，也是扬州现存规模最大的私家园林，她继承了中国传统造园艺术的精华，在中国古典私家园林中具有极高的典型性和代表性。何园规模宏大，包含了中国古典园林的所有要素，并且在园林假山、建筑设计方面具有独到之处，这为我们测试新型数字化测绘技术提供了较好的条件。扬州地方上的园林历史研究有较为深厚的积累，是考察和测绘何园的重要理论基础。何园目前管理体系完善，保护状态比较好，具备数字化测绘现场工作的条件。2018年年底，我们确定了测绘何园的计划，并受到了扬州何园管理处的大力支持。

扬州何园图录项目历时一年，包含案头研究、现场测绘、数据整理、成果编制四个基本阶段。项目团队成员包含园林专家、建筑专家、数字测绘专家、风景园林专业学生志愿者和地方历史学家。团队于2018年年底开展了为期3个月的历史信息收集和整理工作，撰写了何园历史沿革和园林特征等章节的初稿，确定了测绘的范围和重点要素。团队于2018年12月和2019年6月先后两次赴何园开展数字化测绘，为期共15天，采用数字化点云技术对何园的周边环境、园林布局、池山地形、花木建筑等内容进行了高精度测绘。所采用的设备包括低空摄影无人机、数字化近景摄影测量相机、激光雷达三维扫描仪和虚拟现实建模软件。2019年7—9月，项目团队进行了为期3个月的数据处理和分析，生成和绘制了图录的主要照片、模型和测绘图纸。2019年10—12月将图录汇编成册，并配以相应的文字、图片，由此形成了这本《数字化园林遗产图录：扬州何园》的初稿。

《数字化园林遗产图录：扬州何园》包含何园的历史沿革、整体特征、园景及构成要素三个部分，内容以测绘图、航拍影像、现场照片和辅以一定的文字说明的分析图为主。所有测绘图表达的是文化遗产当前的状态，其中既包含各个时期历史要素的叠加，也包含当代的修复、重建、拆除等改动信息。相应章节阐释了园林的变迁和保护历史。书中大量测绘图纸、航拍影像、历史资料均为首次公开发表，高精度点云影像作为主要的图示方式，更好地表达了遗产的特征和细节。同时，我们从数字化模型中提取了何园的二维线划平面图，以便与现有图纸对接。由于目前技术的限制，纸质出版物仍是最为可靠的信息传播媒介之一，因此本书仍旧采用传统的纸质出版物的方式，并设定了240毫米见方的中等开本。

本书所涉的测绘工作受到扬州何园管理处负责人徐亮先生的帮助，也得到赵丹、余德喜等多位管理人员的支持；在何园历史研究过程中，同济大学建筑与城市规划学院朱宇晖老师提供了重要资料；同济大学建筑设计研究院（集团）有限公司和上海建筑数字建造工程技术研究中心为何园测绘项目的数据分析提供了空间和设备支持。在此一并致谢！

the garden at the end of 2018, and received strong support from the local management office.

The digital document project of Heyuan Garden lasted for one year and consisted of 4 main stages: desk research, site mapping, data collation, and results production. Project team members include garden experts, architecture experts, digital surveying experts, landscape garden student volunteers and local historians. At the end of 2018, the team carried out a three-month collection of historical information and compiled the first draft of the chapters on the garden history and character. The scope and key elements of the survey were then identified. The team went to Heyuan Garden twice in December 2018 and June 2019 to carry out digital mapping for a total of 15 days. The digital point cloud technology was used to capture the environment, garden layout, landform, water, buildings and plants by high precision mapping. The equipment used includes low-altitude photography drones, digital close-range photogrammetry cameras, laser scanners, virtual reality modeling software, and so on. From July to September 2019, the project team conducted a three-month data processing and analysis to generate photos, models and maps in a digital format. From October to December 2019, the digital maps, the corresponding texts and photographs were compiled into a book — *Garden Heritage Digital Document: Heyuan Garden / Yangzhou*.

This book contains the thorough description and representation of the evolution, the overall characteristics, and the contributing garden components. It mainly uses maps, aerial photographs, live photos and diagrams with a certain text description. All visual representations reflect the current state of cultural heritage, including the superposition of historical elements of each period, as well as contemporary restoration, reconstruction, demolition and other changes. The evolution and the conservation history for different sections are explained by the text. Many maps, images, aerial photos, and historical material in this book are all published for the first time. The book uses high-precision point cloud images as the main graphical method, which can express more garden detail and character than the traditional two-dimensional line graphics. At the same time, in order to provide better demonstrations and to interface with the existing drawings, we extracted the two-dimensional line graphics of the garden from the digital models. Due to current technical limitations, paper publications are still one of the most reliable media, so this digital document still uses traditional paper publications and sets a moderate format of 240mm square.

The undertaking and completion of the survey work was assisted by Mr. Xu Liang, the director of the Management Office of Heyuan Garden, Ms. Zhao Dan, Mr. Yu Dexi, and other staff of the local management team. The historic research was supported by Dr. Zhu Yuhui from the College of Architecture and Urban Planning in Tongji University. Tongji Architetcural Design (Group) Co., Ltd., and Shanghai Digital Architecture Fabrication Engineering Technology Center (SFAB) provided spaces and facilities for the data analysis of the digital survey. The authors are very grateful for the help provided by these individuals and groups.

05 何园概况
Heyuan Garden Profile

何园位于扬州市明清古城东南部，是一座建成于19世纪的中国古典住宅园林，其原名"寄啸山庄"，取自东晋诗人陶渊明诗句"倚南窗以寄傲""登东皋以舒啸"，隐喻园主对当时清廷朝政的不满，表达隐居避世、寄情山水的初衷。何园是中国封建社会晚期扬州大型园林最后的作品，也是扬州现存规模最大的私家住宅园林，被称作"晚清第一园"。何园继承了中国传统造园艺术的精华，不仅在风格上南北兼具，在建筑细部上也融入西洋元素，形成其特有的园林面貌，在中国古典园林中具有独特的地位和价值。目前，何园作为全国重点文物保护单位对公众开放，是扬州最具代表性的景点之一。

Located in the southeastern part of Ming Qing Historic Town precinct (the construction of which can be traced back to the Ming and Qing dynasties), Yangzhou, Jiangsu Province, China, Heyuan Garden is a Chinese classical residential garden built in the 19th century. It was originally called 'Jixiao Shanzhuang' (Whistling Scholar's Mountain Retreat). The name was taken from the verse lines 'to express my pride leaning on the south window', 'to express my indignation on the eastern hill' by the poet Tao Yuanming in the Eastern Jin dynasty. The name was used to metaphorise the garden owner's dissatisfaction with the Qing government at that time, and expressed his original intention of seclusion and his sentiments vested in mountains and rivers. Heyuan Garden is believed to be Yang-

17　中国江苏省扬州市区位
Location of Yangzhou, Jiangsu Province, China

zhou's last sizeable garden dating back to the Qing dynasty. It is also the largest existing private garden in Yangzhou. It is called the 'First Garden in the Late Qing Dynasty'. Heyuan Garden inherits the essence of Chinese traditional garden art. It not only has a combination of styles in the north and south, but also incorporates foreign elements in the architectural details to form its unique garden appearance, which has unique status and value in Chinese classical gardens. At present, Heyuan Garden is open to the public as a National Key Cultural Relics Protection Unit and is one of the most representative scenic spots in Yangzhou.

遗产名称：
何园（寄啸山庄）
位置：
中国江苏省扬州市徐凝门大街66号
坐标：
东经119°26'36"，北纬32°23'15"
总面积：
1.15公顷
保护等级：
全国重点文物保护单位
保护及管理部门：
扬州何园管理处

Name of the property:
Heyuan Garden ('Jixiao Shangzhuang' in Chinese, i.e. Whistling Scholar's Mountain Retreat)
Location:
No. 66 Xuningmen Street, Yangzhou, Jiangsu Province, China
Geographical coordinates:
32°23'15"N, 119°26'36"E
Area of the property:
1.15 ha
Legal status:
National Key Cultural Relics Protection Unit
Institutions in charge of its management and conservation:
Management Office of Heyuan Garden, Yangzhou

18 何园航拍图 于2019年6月
Aerial photo a of Heyuan Garden, June 2019

06 何园历史沿革
Heyuan Garden History

唐、宋、元以来，中国的江南地区经济繁荣、人文荟萃，一直是传统私家造园最为集中的区域。明清时期，扬州作为中国经济和文化最为发达的城市之一，逐渐成为江南造园活动的中心。清代文人刘大观（1753—1834）提出"杭州以湖山胜，苏州以市肆胜，扬州以园亭胜，三者鼎峙，不可轩轾"的观点，说明当时扬州在园林建设的数量和水平上位居全国之冠。扬州地处长江北岸、江淮平原南端，气候温和、四季分明、水系发达、土壤肥沃，为造园提供了良好的自然条件。同时，扬州又位于长江与京杭大运河的交汇点上，自古便有"楚尾吴头，江淮名邑"之称，独特的地理位置决定了扬州在政治、军事和经济上的重要地位。因其便利的水路交通，扬州曾经是中国粮食、食盐和铁等重要物资的主要集散地，隋唐以后是中国对外贸易的主要港埠。

清代中叶，扬州的经济发展达到顶峰，其城市建设也受到多元文化的影响，来自全国各地的商人聚集扬州，利用经商获取的大量资金大举建造住宅和园林。乾隆皇帝六次南巡均驻跸扬州，当地绅商为了争获皇室青睐，更是大肆兴建园林，形成了中国古代封建社会园林建设的一个"黄金时代"。清代乾隆以后，中国的封建社会开始逐渐走向衰落。清道光年间，由于盐业政策的改变，盐商们失去垄断地位，逐步无利可图，坐吃山空，园林建造和养护失去了经济来源，城内外的大型园林逐渐凋敝。清咸丰年间，太平军三次攻入扬州，战争对扬州园林造成毁灭性的破坏。清"同光中兴"期间，扬州盐业经济稍有复苏，正是在此社会背景下，何园建成于清代晚期，为中国封建社会末期扬州的最后一个大型私家园林作品。其在旧园的基础上改建，历史可以追溯到清代康熙中后期，园史超过三百年，可以分为以下四个时期。

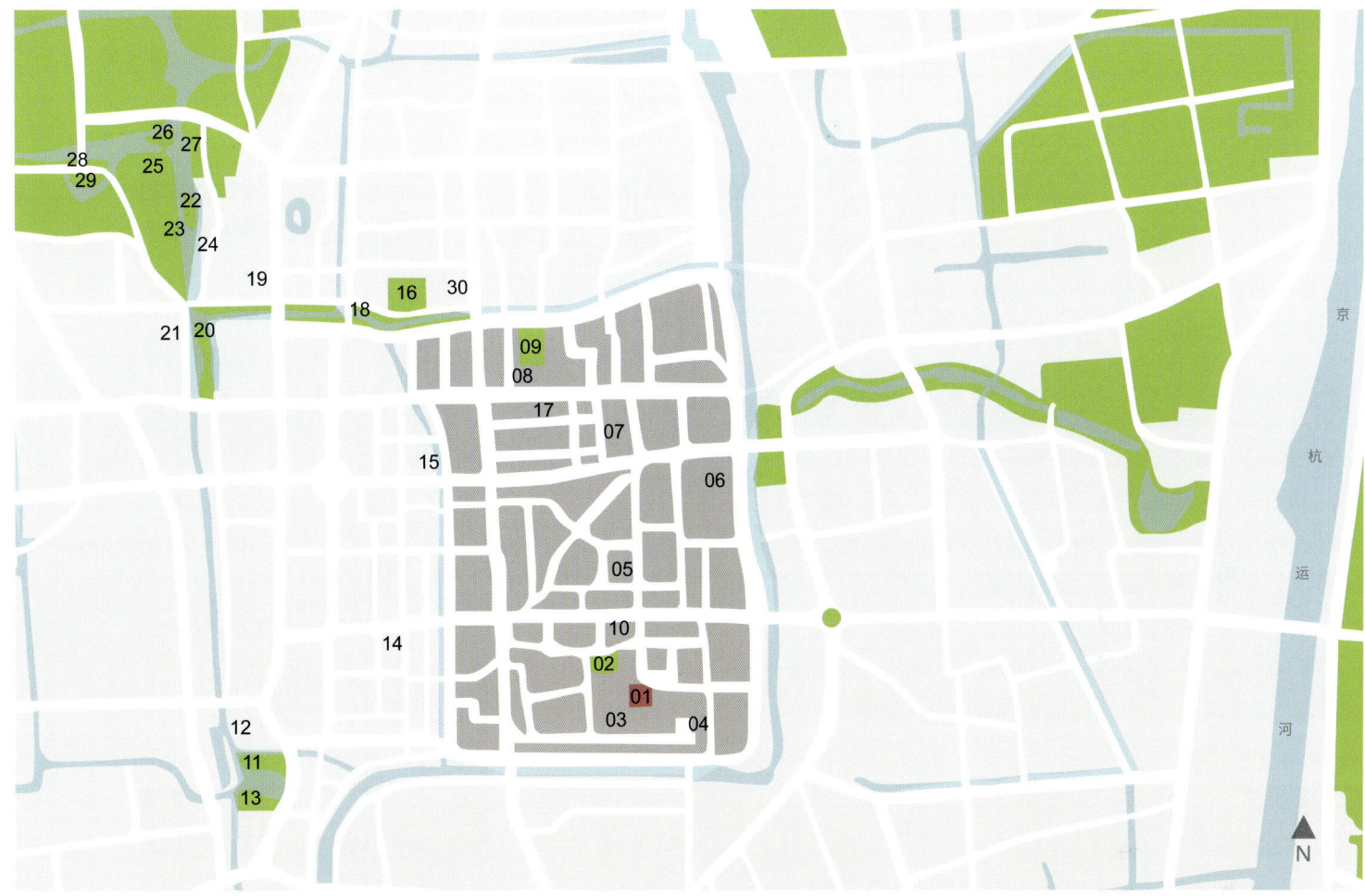

01 何园 Heyuan Garden	09 个园 Geyuan Garden	17 华氏园 Hua's Garden	24 趣园 Quyuan Garden
02 小盘谷 Xiaopangu Garden (Small Meandering Valley)	10 二分明月楼 Erfen Mingyue Building (Loft of Two-Thirds Bright Moonlight)	18 冶春园 Yechun Garden	25 徐园 Xuyuan Garden
03 棣园 (旧址) Diyuan Garden (site)	11 九峰园 Jiufeng Garden	19 卷石洞天 Quanshi Dongtian (Rolling Stone Cavern)	26 小金山 Xiaojinshan Garden (Lesser Golden Hill)
04 卢氏盐商住宅 Salt Merchant Lu Shaoxu's House	12 影园 (旧址) Yingyuan Garden (site)	20 倚虹园(旧址) Yihong Garden (site)	27 四桥烟雨 Siqiao Yanyu (Mist and Rain over Four Bridges)
05 蔚圃 Weipu Garden	13 荷花池公园 Lotus Pond Park	21 虹桥修禊 (旧址) Hongqiao Xiuxi (Venue for Spring Outings at the Rainbow Bridge, site)	28 白塔晴云 Baita Qingyun (White Stupa under Clear Clouds)
06 吴道台宅第 Wu Yinsun's Mansion	14 鲍庐 Paolu Garden	22 荷蒲熏风 Hepu Xunfeng (Lotus-Scented Breeze Garden)	29 莲性寺 Lianxing Temple
07 汪氏小苑 Wang Zhuming's Little Garden	15 珍园 Zhenyuan Garden	23 长堤春柳 Changdi Chunliu (Long Dyke Flanked by Spring Willows)	30 史公祠 Shi Kefa Memorial Hall
08 逸圃 Yipu Garden	16 天宁寺 Tianning Temple		

19 扬州古城区古典园林分布图
The classical gardens in the historic town of Yangzhou

片石山房时期（约清康熙中后期—1882年）

已知记载中，何园的历史最早可以追溯至清代康熙年间的吴家龙别业。康熙中后期，徽州商人吴家龙在扬州新城东南部修筑了一座别业，其范围南至花园巷，北至刁家巷，即今日何园的大致范围。因别业中有两棵古槐树，因此又名"双槐园"。据笔记小说《花间笑语》记载，双槐园内主要有听雨轩、瓶榴斋、蝴蝶厅、梅楼、水榭等建筑，以及假山和水池等园景。其中一座著名的太湖石假山被清代文人钱泳认为是清代大画家石涛的作品，名为"片石山房"。但《花间笑语》指出，园林中的假山是由扬州莲性寺牧山和尚设计。乾隆后期，别业传至吴家龙之孙吴之黼，至嘉庆中后期，园林已逐渐荒废。道光年间，片石山房假山及其周边区域为一媒婆所得，改称"双槐茶园"，假山前的水池由曲池改为方池，面积缩小，周围建筑改造为戏园式样，用于开设面馆，兼为卖戏之所。同治年间至光绪初年，粤人吴辉谟购此花园，经修葺后作为居所，直到光绪九年（1883）何氏入住并修建寄啸山庄。

由于年代久远，吴家龙别业的具体范围已经无法确定，但一些园景及要素保留至今，有助于我们判断别业的大致规模。两棵古槐树20世纪60年代以前仍存于今日何园船厅（桴海轩）南侧，后因养护不善而枯死；1962年，同济大学园林专家陈从周通过文献考证和实地勘察，判断今日何园东南部的片石山房假山即为画家石涛的作品，是吴氏别业的重要组成部分；另据扬州古建筑专家赵立昌先生考证，今日何园北部的蝴蝶厅、船厅等均为清代前期与中期的建筑形制，极有可能是吴氏别业的遗存。另外，片石山房假山西侧的骑马楼、东二楼、东三楼，墙体多用旧砖，据推测可能是吴辉谟在双槐园的梅楼旧址上建造的。

寄啸山庄时期（1883—1944年）

何园的主人是清代光绪年间的官员何维键。何维键（1835—1908），字汝持，号芷舠，安徽望江人，曾

20 片石山房太湖石假山，2019年6月
Taihu Lake stone rockery in the Small-Rock Mountain Retreat, June 2019

Since the Tang, Song and Yuan dynasties, the economy and culture of China's Jiangnan area has prospered, and has always had the highest concentration of traditional private gardens. During the Ming and Qing dynasties, Yangzhou, as one of the most developed cities in China, gradually became the centre of Jiangnan's gardening activities. Liu Daguan (1753–1834), a scholar in the Qing dynasty, put forward the view that 'Hangzhou puts its name on the map with its lakes and mountains, and Suzhou does so with its markets and shops, whereas Yangzhou excels with its gardens. The three cities face each other like the legs of a tripod — there is no telling which city is the best', indicating that Yangzhou ranked highest in number and quality of garden construction. Yangzhou is located on the north bank of the Yangtze River and at the southern end of the Jianghuai Plain. The climate is mild, the four seasons are distinct, the water system is developed, and the soil is fertile, providing good natural conditions for gardening. At the same time, Yangzhou is located at the intersection of the Yangtze River and the Beijing-Hangzhou Grand Canal. Since ancient times, it has been known as 'the tail of Chu State and the head of Wu State, and the most famous city in the Jianghuai Plain'. The unique geographical location determines the important status of Yangzhou in politics, economics and military power. Because of its convenient waterway transportation, Yangzhou was once the main distribution centre for important resources such as grain, salt and iron in China. After the Sui and Tang dynasties, it was the main port of China's foreign trade.

In the middle of the Qing dynasty, Yangzhou's economic development reached its peak. Its urban construction was influenced by multiculturalism. Merchants from all over the country gathered in Yangzhou, using the significant funds acquired in business to build houses and gardens on a large scale. The Emperor Qianlong had six southern inspection tours to Yangzhou. To curry favour with the imperial family, local gentry and merchants joined in the garden-building frenzy and constructed many gardens, establishing a 'golden age' of garden development in ancient Chinese feudal society. After the Qianlong reign of the Qing dynasty, China's feudal society began to gradually decline, and the Western capitalist powers became increasingly influential. With the changes in salt industry policy during the Daoguang reign of the Qing dynasty, the salt trade became unprofitable, garden construction and maintenance lost economic resources, and the large gardens in the city gradually faded. During the Xianfeng reign, the Taiping Army invaded Yangzhou three times, and the war caused devastating damage to the gardens of Yangzhou. During the brief prosperity in Tongzhi and Guangxu reigns, Yangzhou's salt economy slightly recovered. It was in this social background that Heyuan Garden was built and it was the last large private garden in Yangzhou in the late feudal society. It was built based on a historic garden and its history can be traced back to the second half of the Kangxi reign. The garden has a history of more than 300 years, falling into the following four periods.

The period of the Small-Rock Mountain Retreat (about the 2nd half of the Kangxi reign of the Qing dynasty–1882)

In the known records, the history of Heyuan Garden can be traced back to Wu Jialong's villa in the Kangxi reign. Around the second half of the Kangxi reign (1703), Huizhou merchant Wu Jialong built a villa in the southeast of Yangzhou new town. The villa extended north to Diaojia Lane and south to

21 何维键全身像，约翰·汤姆森摄于1869年，现藏于伦敦维尔康姆收藏馆
He Weijian portrait, photograph by John Thomson, 1869, Wellcome Collection, London, UK

Huayuan Lane. This remains the approximate extent of Heyuan Garden today. Because there were two ancient pagoda trees in the villa, the garden is also known as 'Shuanghuai Yuan' (Twin Pagoda Trees Garden). According to the collection of short stories *Huajian Xiaoyu* (Banters amidst flowers), there were Tingyu Pavilion, Pinglei Building, Butterfly Hall, Meilou Building, water-front gazebo, as well as rockeries and ponds in the garden. There was a famous artificial Taihu Lake stone mountain in the garden. Qian Yong, one of the literati in the Qing dynasty said this artificial mountain was designed by Shitao, the great artist of the Qing dynasty. The artificial mountain is called 'Pianshi Shanfang' (Small-Rock Mountain Retreat). However, *Huajian Xiaoyu* pointed out that the artificial mountain in the Twin Pagoda Trees Garden was designed by a monk of Lianxing Temple in Yangzhou during the Qianlong reign. In the late Qianlong reign, the villa was passed to Wu Zhifu, the grandson of Wu Jialong. In the middle and late Jiaqing reign, the garden was gradually abandoned. During the Daoguang reign, the famous artificial Taihu Lake stone mountain and its surrounding areas were acquired by a matchmaker. It was renamed 'Shuanghuai Chayuan' (Twin Pagoda Trees Tea Garden). The pond in front of the rockery was changed from an irregular shape to a rectangle, the area was reduced, and the surrounding buildings were transformed into a theatre style for the opening of the noodle restaurant and a place for performing traditional Chinese opera as well. From Tongzhi to early Guangxu reign, Wu Huimo, a Cantonese purchased this garden and lived there after repairs, until He's family moved in and built Whistling Scholar's Mountain Retreat in the ninth year of the Guangxu reign (1883).

Due to age, the specific extent of Wu Jialong's villa cannot be determined, but some landscape and elements remain to this day. This helps us to estimate the approximate scale. The two ancient pagoda trees were still alive on the south side of the Boat Hall (Fuhai Hall) until the 1960s, but died due to poor maintenance. Chen Congzhou, a garden expert of Tongji University, discovered an artificial Taihu Lake stone mountain in the southeast part of Heyuan Garden in 1962. Based on the literature research and site investigation, he judged that this piece of artificial mountain, named Small-Rock Mountain Retreat, is the work of the famous artist Shitao, and is part of the Twin Pagoda Trees Garden. According to Yangzhou ancient architecture expert Zhao Lichang, the Butterfly Hall and the Boat Hall in the north of Heyuan Garden are all in the style of the early and middle of the Qing dynasty. Therefore, they are likely to be the remains of Wu Jialong's villa. In addition, the west side of Small-Rock Mountain Retreat is the Qima Building (Riding-Horse Building), the Second East Building, and the Third East Building. Many of the walls were made of old bricks. It is speculated that Wu Huimo built these buildings based on the historic site of Meilou Building in the Twin Pagoda Trees Garden.

The period of the Whistling Scholar's Mountain Retreat (1883–1944)

The first owner of Heyuan Garden was He Weijian (1835–1908), style name Ruchi, pseudonym Zhidao, a native of Wangjiang, Anhui. He Weijian was an official under the Guangxu reign of the Qing dynasty. He used to serve as the director of the Ministry of Revenue, in charge of Yunan and Fujian. Later he was transferred to Hubei as an intendant of a circuit (an administrative division) to host the Bureau

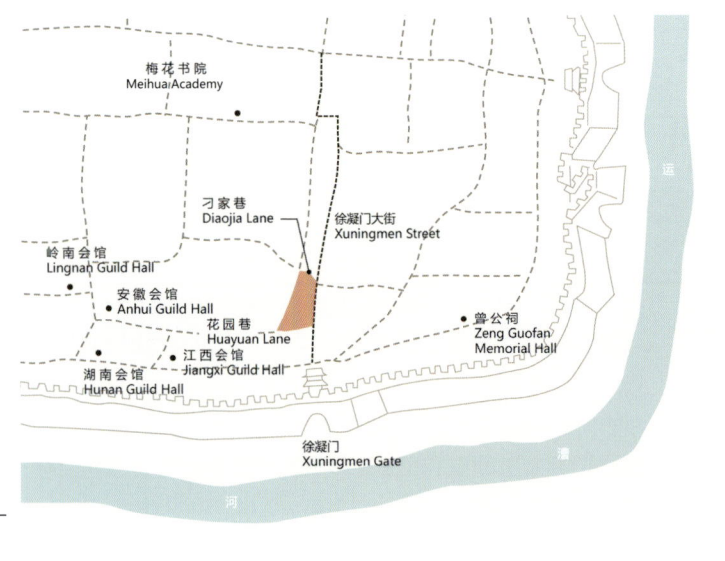
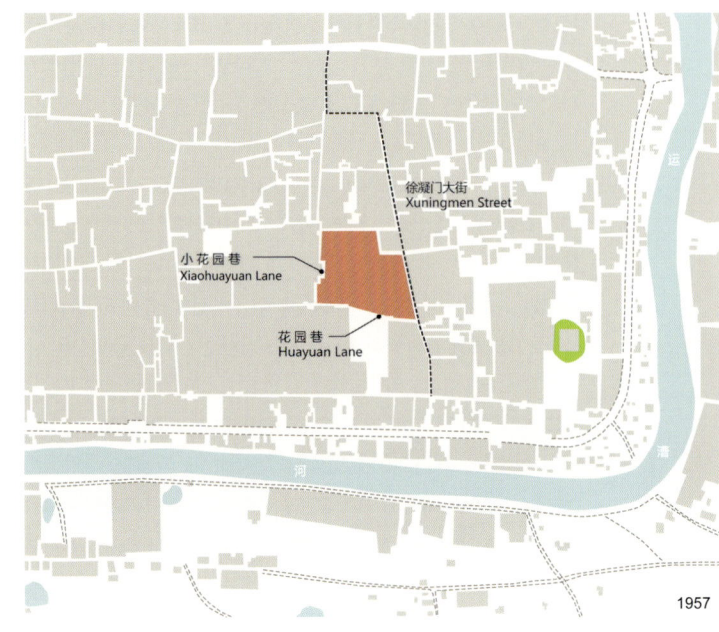

1871—1908

1957

任户部郎中，分管福建司、云南司，后改任道员，分发到湖北，主办军需局，此后两次代理盐法道，补任督粮道，在其担任湖北按察使不久，又接任汉黄德道，并兼任江汉关监督。何维键除了长期在军需、盐运、粮储以及海关等要职上任官以外，也是典型的封建绅商。按照清代晚期的盐法制度，官员从商是合法而且极其普遍的现象，何维键不仅在安徽、江苏和湖北有田地产，还是经营盐票的大盐商，因此得以有充分的财力营建何园。

清代光绪年间，何维键时任汉黄德道，监督江汉关。他看透了清政府对外政策上的软弱和官场上派系林立的纷争，个人夹在矛盾旋涡之中，稍不留神就会被倾轧，因而对仕途心灰意冷。光绪八年（1882），何维键以侍奉生母为由，从任上辞退归隐扬州。次年（1883）购得吴氏双槐园的北部区域，在此基础上修造自己的宅园，并取名"寄啸山庄"表达对当时统治者的不满。何维键对旧址上的建筑和园景要素进行重新整理和组织，拆除了大片的建筑，建造了西洋楼、赏月楼等建筑作为居住空间，构思并设计了北部花园。光绪十年（1884），何维键又购得当年吴辉谟居住的片石山房区域，将该区域的太湖石假山、水池和楠木厅等划分为一个独立的小园，保存其基本格局，后来又在其东部新建了家祠。至此，何园的整体格局基本形成。

光绪二十七年（1901），66岁的何维键举家迁往上海，投资银行、煤铁厂矿公司、学校等事业，何园交给管家看管。1935年，何维键的长子何声灏一家为节省生活开支回到何园居住，直到1937年日本发动全面侵华战争，何声灏一家又逃难到上海。1944年2月，何氏后代回到何园居住，同年5—6月，将何园除片石山房东侧四座院落以外的部分全部出售给了汉奸殷汝耕，并在花园巷另开一扇大门，用砖墙将售出部分隔开，由此结束了何园长达61年的何氏私家宅园的历史。

 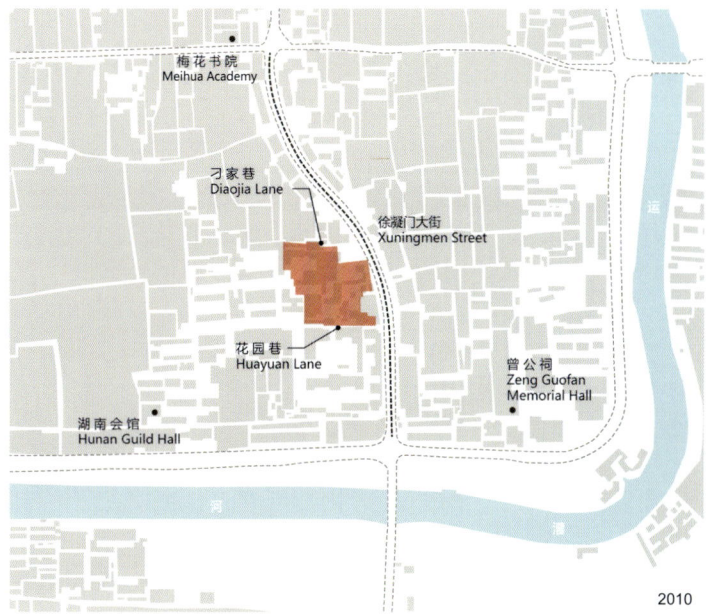

22 何园范围的演变
The evolution of the boundary of Heyuan Garden

of Munition. Then he served as the supervisor of the salt administration, and then grain transportation. As soon as he served as the prosecutor of Hubei, he took over as intendant of Hanhuangde circuits in Hubei, and served as the governor of the General Administrator of Hankou Customs. In addition to long-term positions in military service, salt transportation, grain storage, and customs, He Weijian is also a typical feudal merchant. Under the provisions of the salt law system in the late Qing dynasty, officials commonly and legally engaged in business activities. He Weijian not only had real estate in Anhui, Jiangsu and Hubei, but was also an active salt merchant trading salt voucher. These financial resources enabled him to build a garden.

During the Guangxu reign in the Qing dynasty, He Weijian was the leader of the Hanhuangde government office and supervised Hankou Customs. He saw the humiliation of the Qing government's foreign policy and the factional strife in the officialdom. He was caught in the vortex of contradiction, and would be crushed if he didn't pay attention. He was disheartened by his career. In the eighth year of the Guangxu reign (1882), He Weijian resigned and returned to Yangzhou using the excuse that he had to look after his mother. In the following year (1883), he purchased the northern part of Wu's Twin Pagoda Trees Garden and built his own family garden based on the earlier work. The main garden precinct was named 'Jingxiao Shanzhuang' (Whistling Scholar's Mountain Retreat) to express his dissatisfaction with the rulers of the time. He Weijian reorganised the architectural and landscape elements on the site, demolished many buildings, built buildings such as the Western-Style Building and Shangyue Building (Moon-Viewing Building) as residential spaces, and conceived and designed the northern garden. In

23 何维键的第四代嫡孙在蝴蝶厅前合影, 1935年.
来源:扬州何园管理处提供

He Weijian's great-grandsons in front of the Butterfly Hall, 1935.
Source: Management Office of Heyuan Garden, Yangzhou

公共使用时期（1944—1959年）

1945年抗日战争胜利以后，国民党政府以日伪财产接收何园，没收归公，并在此开办了私立祝同中学。1946—1947年，何园由淮安中学使用，其间园林中的许多建筑都被用作教学场地。1950年，中国人民解放军苏北军区医院进驻何园，次年迁至淮安。1953年，江苏省军区文化速成中学进驻何园，之后华东军区第五速成中学、南京军区第五速成中学、部队第二十文化速成中学又先后驻用何园。这一时期园内的古建筑遭到一定程度的损坏。

遗产保护时期（1959年至今）

1959年开始，扬州市政府将何园北部园林部分交给市园林管理部门整修并于10月1日将其对外开放。1962年5月，扬州市人民委员会将何园（寄啸山庄）列为文物保护单位。1963年，后花园及祠堂以外部分交给国防部第七研究所驻用，之后又先后为六机部七院第五研究所（705所）、六机部七院第十研究院（710所）所驻用。1969年，扬州市革命委员会将何园园林部分交给扬州无线电厂，其中一些主要厅馆用作车间，由于缺少养护，导致一些古树死亡。1972年，六机部七院第二十三研究所（723所）由青岛迁至扬州，利用何园内

the tenth year of Guangxu reign (1884), He Weijian purchased the artificial Taihu Lake stone mountain area (i.e. Small-Rock Mountain Retreat) where Wu Huimo lived, and made it an independent small garden. The Ancestor Hall of He's family was then built in the east. At this point, the overall pattern of Heyuan Garden had been established.

In the twenty-seventh year of the Guangxu reign (1901), 66-year-old He Weijian moved his family to Shanghai to invest in banking, a coal-iron plant, a mining company, a school and other businesses. Heyuan Garden was handed over to a housekeeper. He Weijian's eldest son, He Shenghao, returned to Heyuan Garden in 1935 to reduce his living expenses. When Japan launched a full-scale invasion of China in 1937, He Shenghao fled to Shanghai again. In 1944, the descendants of He returned to Heyuan Garden. In the same year, they sold all the parts of the garden except the four courtyards on the east side of the Small-Rock Mountain Retreat to the traitor Yin Rugeng, and opened another gate in Huayuan Lane. The two compartments were separated by a new brick wall, which ended the history of what had been He's private homestead for 61 years.

The period of public use (1944–1959)

After the victory of the War of Resistance against Japanese Aggression in 1945, the Kuomintang government reclaimed the garden as a property from the puppet government of Japan. The confiscated garden was returned to the public and was used to accommodate the private Zhutong Middle School. In 1946–1947, Heyuan Garden was then used by Huai'an Middle School. During this period many buildings in the garden were used as teaching spaces. In 1950, the People's Liberation Army's Subei Military Region Hospital was stationed in Heyuan Garden, but then moved to Huai'an in the following year. In 1953, the Jiangsu Province Military Region Culture Accelerated Middle School entered Heyuan Garden, and then the Fifth Accelerated Middle School of the East China Military Region, the Fifth Accelerated Middle School of the Nanjing Military Region, and the 20th Accelerated Middle School of the Forces were successively stationed there. The occupation led to some damage of the historic buildings.

The period of cultural heritage conservation (1959–present)

Beginning in 1959, the Yangzhou Municipal Government handed over the northern part of Heyuan Garden to the city's garden management department for renovation and opened this part to the public on 1 October. Heyuan Garden was listed as the municipal cultural heritage site by the People's Committee of Yangzhou in May 1962. In 1963, the majority of the garden except the northern precinct and the ancestral hall was handed over to the Seventh Research Institute of the Ministry of National Defense. Later, it was successively used by the Fifth Research Institute and the Tenth Research Institute of the Seventh Academy of the Sixth Ministry of Mechanical Industry (Institute 705 and Institute 710). In 1969, the Yangzhou Revolutionary Committee handed over the northern part of garden to the Yangzhou Radio Factory. Some of the main halls were used as workshops, and some old trees died due to lack of maintenance. In 1972, the Twenty-third Research Institute of the Seventh Academy of the Sixth Ministry of Mechanical Industry (Insti-

710所的营房开展工作。1979年，扬州无线电厂搬出，但这十年对园林部分造成了比较大的破坏，许多假山石用于铺路，园林内部陈设散失，仅存北部与西侧花园比较完整，片石山房太湖石假山仅保留了西侧的主峰、东部部分残石以及一株罗汉松。

1979年后，何园北部园林部分重新交给扬州市园林管理部门整修，修复了假山、曲池、厅堂楼阁，补植了大量树木花卉，并重新向公众开放。1982年，何园被列入江苏省省级文物保护单位名单，这是其保护历史上的重要里程碑。同年，何园园居部分以及片石山房花园由723所移交给扬州市园林管理部门进行整修和保护。1986年，何园在东侧徐凝门大街新开辟主要出入口。1988年，何园被国务院公布为第三批全国重点文物保护单位。1989年，片石山房区域得到整修，修复了太湖石假山、曲池和楠木厅，并增建了部分建筑从而形成完整的园林院落。同年，何园南门得到恢复。2002年，园居部分的西洋楼北楼经修复后对外开放，次年又修复了东二楼、东三楼，并将西洋楼南楼维修后对外开放。2007年园林管理部门收回了何家祠堂，加之整修后对外开放，至此形成何园今日的面貌。

tute 723) moved from Qingdao to Yangzhou, using Heyuan Garden as its offices. In 1979, Yangzhou Radio Factory moved out, but during the previous ten years had caused great damage to the garden. Many of the artificial rockeries had been smashed, the broken stone were used for road paving, and the interior furnishings of the garden were lost. Only the remaining garden areas in the north and west sides were relatively complete. In the famous artificial Taihu Lake stone mountain, only the main peak on the west side, the cave on the east, and an old *podocarpus macrophyllus* survived.

After 1979, the northern part of Heyuan Garden was re-submitted to the city's garden management department for restoration. The rockery, pond, and many buildings were restored. Many trees and flowers were replanted. The garden was opened to the public again. In 1982, Heyuan Garden was listed as a provincial-level cultural relics protection unit of Jiangsu Province. This was an important milestone in its conservation. In the same year, the residential area of Heyuan Garden and the area of Small-Rock Mountain Retreat were handed over to the garden management department of Yangzhou for heritage conservation. In 1986, a new entrance was built on the east side of Heyuan Garden on Xuningmen Street. In 1988, Heyuan Garden was announced by the State Council as the third batch of National Key Cultural Relics Protection Unit. In 1989, the area of Small-Rock Mountain Retreat was repaired, and the artificial Taihu Lake stone mountain, the pond, and the Phoebe nanmu Hall were restored. Some new buildings were built to form a complete courtyard. In the same year, the south gate of Heyuan Garden was restored. In 2002, the north block of the Western-Style Building in the residential area was repaired and opened to the public. The following year, the Second East Building and the Third East Building were restored, and the south block of the Western-Style Building was repaired and opened to the public. In 2007, the garden management department took back the Ancestor Hall of the He family and opened it to the public after restoration. All of this history and these works have contributed to the appearance of Heyuan Garden today.

07 何园整体特征
Heyuan Garden Character

何园作为一处有意设计的景观，有其明确的立意、构思、布局，虽历经百余年的沧桑变化，其整体特征至今仍清晰可辨，将其置于中国古典园林体系中审视，仍独具特色。由于地处中国南方和北方之间，扬州的园林风格融合了北方园林与江南私家园林的特征，展现出独特的面貌。著名园林专家陈从周先生指出："扬州园林综合了南北的特色，自成一格，雄伟中寓明秀，得雅健之致。"扬州园林多与住宅很好地结合，大多园林中部建造水池，水池旁边堆叠假山，厅堂位于水池边的重要位置，周围点缀亭台楼阁等建筑，并以花墙山石、树木花卉形成园林之间的间隔，创造具有层次变化的景色。清代中叶，扬州园林的主人大多为富商，园林不仅是他们居住的场所，更是展示富有、追求风雅的社交空间，因此在风格、材料和工艺上极为注重奢华，建筑高敞华丽，花木品类丰富，室内外装修精致，叠石筑山的造诣尤其突出。清代乾隆年间成书的《扬州画舫录》就有"扬州以名园胜，名园以叠石胜"的评价。此外，清代的扬州是中国对外贸易的主要商业城市之一，商业上的交往使得许多西方园林、建筑的做法传入并被吸收到扬州园林之中，形成了私家园林中西合璧的独特风貌。何园作为一处晚清扬州私家住宅园林，具有以下突出特征。

寄情山水，以小寓大

营造园林意境是中国古典园林审美的最高标准，园林中的山池花木、亭台楼阁，每一处景物都需要传达造园者的情感和精神追求。何园的整体构思和园林营建充分体现了中国古典园林的这一特性，园林意境突出、景观象征性丰富。园主何维键在任时目睹清朝衰败屈从外强，辞官卸任后建造园林以寄情山水，并将其命名为"寄啸山庄"以表达对清廷朝政的不满。所谓"山庄"，即是一座以古代"海上仙山"传说为蓝本营建的园林。何园的主花园利用水池象征茫茫大海，池西堆筑湖石假山象

24 何园航拍图-b，2018年12月
Aerial photo-b of Heyuan Garden, December 2018

As a designed landscape, Heyuan Garden has clear concept, design and layout. Although it has been subject to more than one hundred years of change, its overall characteristics are still clearly identifiable. The character of Heyuan Garden demonstrates many innovations in the craft of landscape gardening. Due to its location between southern and northern China, Yangzhou's garden style combines the characteristics of northern gardens and private gardens in Jiangnan area, showing a unique look. The famous garden expert Chen Congzhou pointed out: 'Yangzhou gardens become a school. They entail dainty gracefulness in magnificent bodies — or, in literary jargon, write subtle heartthrobs with a robust brush.' Yangzhou gardens are well integrated with residential buildings. Most large gardens in Yangzhou feature a pond in the centre while pavilions become architectural centrepieces. The relationship between ponds and pavilions must be carefully choreographed. The scenery in large gardens is segmented with walls, rockwork and trees to conjure up multi-layered and variegated views. Exotic rocks are erected by the pond, pavilions and belvederes are scattered but ultimately connected by a circuitous walkway. In the middle of the Qing dynasty, most of the owners of Yangzhou gardens

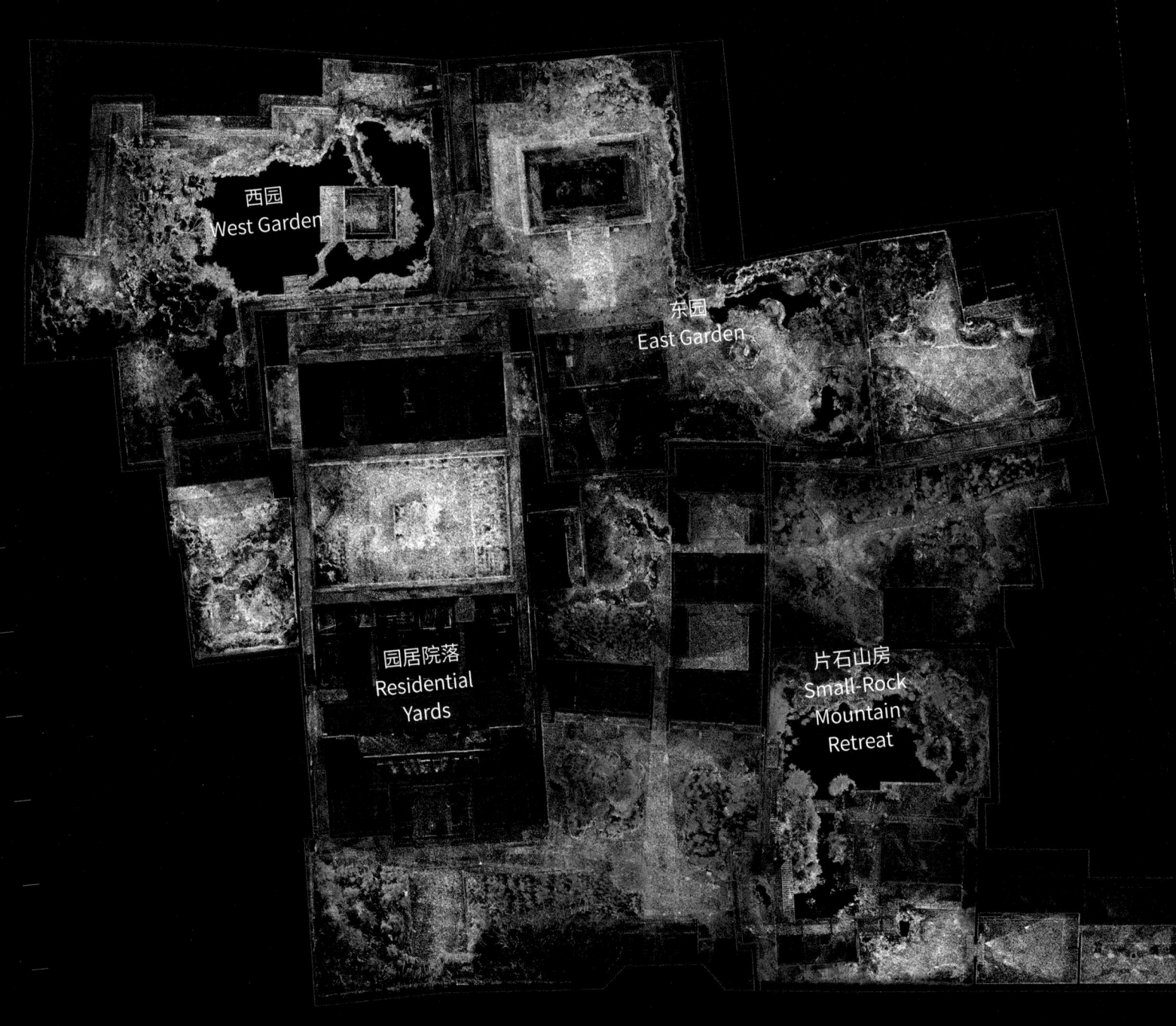

26 何园一层平面图
Ground floor plan of Heyuan Garden

征海上仙山，假山突出水岸，山上种植两株高大挺拔的白皮松，增加了神山的意境。水池中心建造方亭，被称为"小方壶"，具有海上神山仙阁的寓意。何园东北部还利用"旱园水作"的手法，即利用卵石的纹理变化铺装园林地面，形成"无水但有水意"的景观，地面上有四面通透的建筑，营造船浮于海的意象，与整个园林海上仙山的境界融为一体。此外，在整个何园中，利用花窗泄景、半壁亭台、贴墙作山、环阁凿池等手法，都是希望创造以小寓大，在有限中创造无限的景观效果。

院落重重，以园环居

何园是一处典型的中国古典住宅园林，园林坐北朝南，面积约为1.15万平方米，其中建筑面积约为6000平方米，具有清代中后期私家园林建筑密度较高的特征。何园主要通过院落来组织空间，利用围墙将园林划分成十余个大小不同的庭院，再通过门洞、长廊、花窗等串连交通和引导视线，借助池山、植物创造景观层次，减弱建筑带来的限定感，营造无限的自然境界。整个园林以园居院落为中心，北部布置东、西两座花园，西南有赏月楼小花园，东南有片石山房花园，形成了居住空间居中、山水游赏空间环绕的整体格局。这极大丰富了住宅园林的景观变化，不但继承了中国传统住宅园林"前宅后园"或"宅旁设园"的基本传统，又具有独特性和创造性。

立体交通，居游两宜

何园在处理居与游的关系方面具有独到之处，除了"以园环居"的布局特征之外，另一创造便是全园的立体交通。何园在建造之初就设计了复道回廊，解决了园林内部相互联络的问题，串连了园林的主体建筑和花园，同时提供了半室外的遮风避雨的空间，满足居住者在园内的日常行走需要。复道回廊不仅平面上曲折迂回，立面上也高低错落，创造了重要的观景线路和视角，形成了独特的景观体验，行走在回廊里仿佛置身中国卷轴画中，景观画面依次展开，引人入胜。复道回廊本身也是重要的景观界面，西园中的回廊高两层，环抱水池，加以栏杆、花窗的多样变化，营造了精致典雅的园林立面。长廊是中国传统园林中的重要元素，而何园在继承传统的同时又有所创新，以复道回廊为核心的立体交通系统在中国传统私家园林中别具一格，是江南园林中的孤例。

中西合璧，以人为本

晚清时期，随着中西方文化交流的增多，扬州的园林建筑也受到西方影响。何园主人何维键曾在海关任职并有与洋人共事的经历，因此他在建造何园的时候引入了许多西洋元素，将其与中国传统园林的形制相互融合，更好地满足居住和游赏的需求。这些西洋元素主要体现在西洋楼、煦春堂等建筑上，比如利用百叶窗、壁炉、地下通风穴道等西式元素优化西洋楼的建筑功能，在煦春堂引入玻璃、金属栏杆等新材料作为园林的装饰，形成了新的建筑美学特征。这些元素虽然与中国传统园林的审美有所不同，但无疑是清代晚期西方风格影响下中国古典园林风格的真实写照，从园林发展历史的角度看来，何园是一个十分珍贵的样本。

were rich merchants. The gardens were not only the place where they lived, but also the social space that flaunted wealth and elegance. Therefore, they pursued luxury in style, materials and craftsmanship, and the buildings were spacious and gorgeous, and the flowers and trees were classed. The indoor and outdoor decoration was exquisite, especially the artificial mountains. *Yangzhou Huafang Lu* (The record of the painted pleasure boats of Yangzhou) recorded that, 'Yangzhou makes a name for herself with famed gardens; her gardens put their names on the map with stacked rockwork.' In addition, Yangzhou in the Qing dynasty was one of the major commercial cities for China to operate foreign trade. Commercial exchanges have led to the introduction and absorption of many Western gardens and architectural practices into the local gardening activities, forming a unique style of Yangzhou private gardens. As a private residential garden in Yangzhou built in the late Qing dynasty, Heyuan Garden has the following characteristics.

Idealised miniature landscape and showing the large in the small

To create an artistic conception is the highest standard of Chinese classical garden aesthetics. The artificial mountains, ponds, trees, and buildings need to convey the emotional and spiritual interests of the garden owners. In this way Chinese gardens are idealised miniature (natural) landscapes. The overall concept and construction of Heyuan Garden fully embodies this characteristic of Chinese classical gardens, with outstanding artistic conception and rich symbolic landscape. When He Weijian was in office, he witnessed the decline and submission of the Qing government to Western powers. After resigning, he built a garden as a retreat, and named it Whistling Scholar's Mountain Retreat to express his dissatisfaction with the Qing government. The so-called 'mountain retreat' is a garden built on the Chinese ancient legend of 'sacred mountains in the sea'. The main garden uses the pond to symbolise the sea. The artificial mountain in the west of the pond symbolises the sacred mountains in the sea. The artificial mountain stands out from the waterfront, with two tall white bark pines planted on the mountain, enhancing the atmosphere of the 'sacred mountains'. A square pavilion stands in the east of the pond. It is called 'Xiao Fanghu' (the small square pot, and 'Fanghu' is said to be one sacred mountain's name) in Chinese traditional garden, symbolising the dwelling place for immortals. In addition, the northeastern part of Heyuan Garden uses the method of 'hanyuan shuizuo' (a water-less garden is made to look like water-bound), which uses pavement texture changes to form an imagination of watery landscape with little or no water. A hall with windows on four sides sits in the court. The ground at the foot of the hall's stairway is paved with a mixture of cobbles, broken bricks and tiles in patterns. It aims to create the appearance of a ship floating on the sea. In addition, Heyuan Garden also uses 'borrowed view' lattice windows, half-wall pavilions, wall-mounting mountains, ring-shaped chiseling pools, to create unlimited landscape effects in limited spaces.

Full of courtyards and gardens surrounding residential spaces

Heyuan Garden is a typical Chinese classical residential garden. The garden faces south and covers an area of about 11,500 square metres, including a construction area of about 6,000 square metres. The high density of buildings is a feature of the pri-

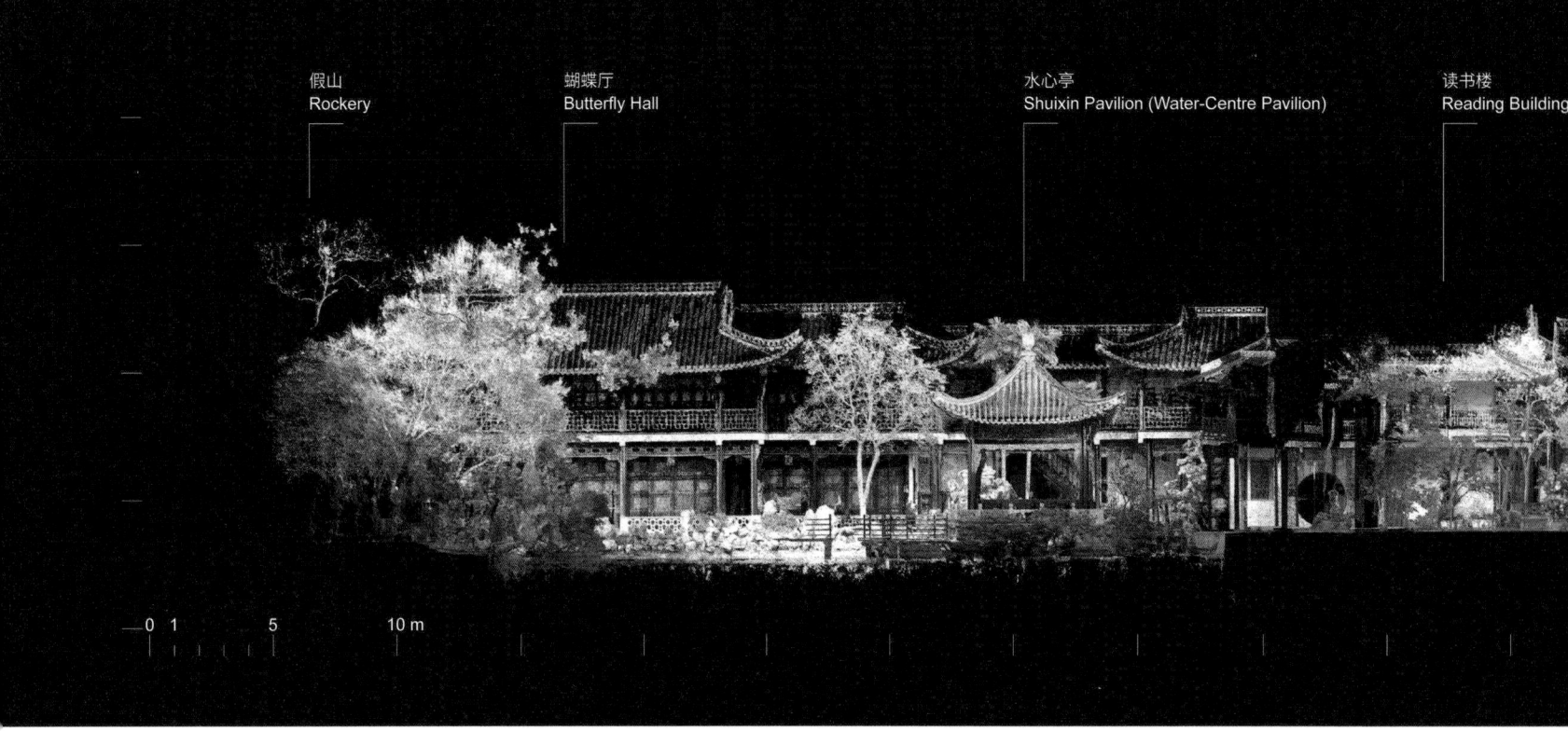

27 何园北部整体剖面图
The overall section of the northern part of Heyuan Garden

vate gardens in the middle and late Qing dynasty. The external space of Heyuan Garden is mainly made up of courtyards. More than ten courtyards of different sizes are created via using walls. Circulation is facilitated through doorways, corridors, lattice windows and other elements to guide the line of sight. Rockeries and pond plants are used to soften the sense of enclosure established by the architecture and to create an infinite natural realm. The residential area is in the centre of the complex, with East and West gardens arranged in the north, Shangyue Building (Moon-Viewing Building) yard in the southwest, and the Small-Rock Mountain Retreat garden in the southeast. This forms the overall pattern of living spaces surrounded by gardens.

The layout positively enriches the landscape experience of the living spaces. Heyuan Garden not only inherits the basic principles of traditional Chinese residential gardens, such as 'front house back garden' or 'garden besides house', but also has its own unique and creative qualities.

The 3D walking system providing spaces for both living and sightseeing

Heyuan Garden is unique in dealing with the relationship between residence and recreation. In addition to the layout feature of 'residential area surrounded by gardens', another creative aspect is the three-dimensional walking system — the Double-Lev-

76
77

28 何园点云模型透视图
Point cloud model of Heyuan Garden

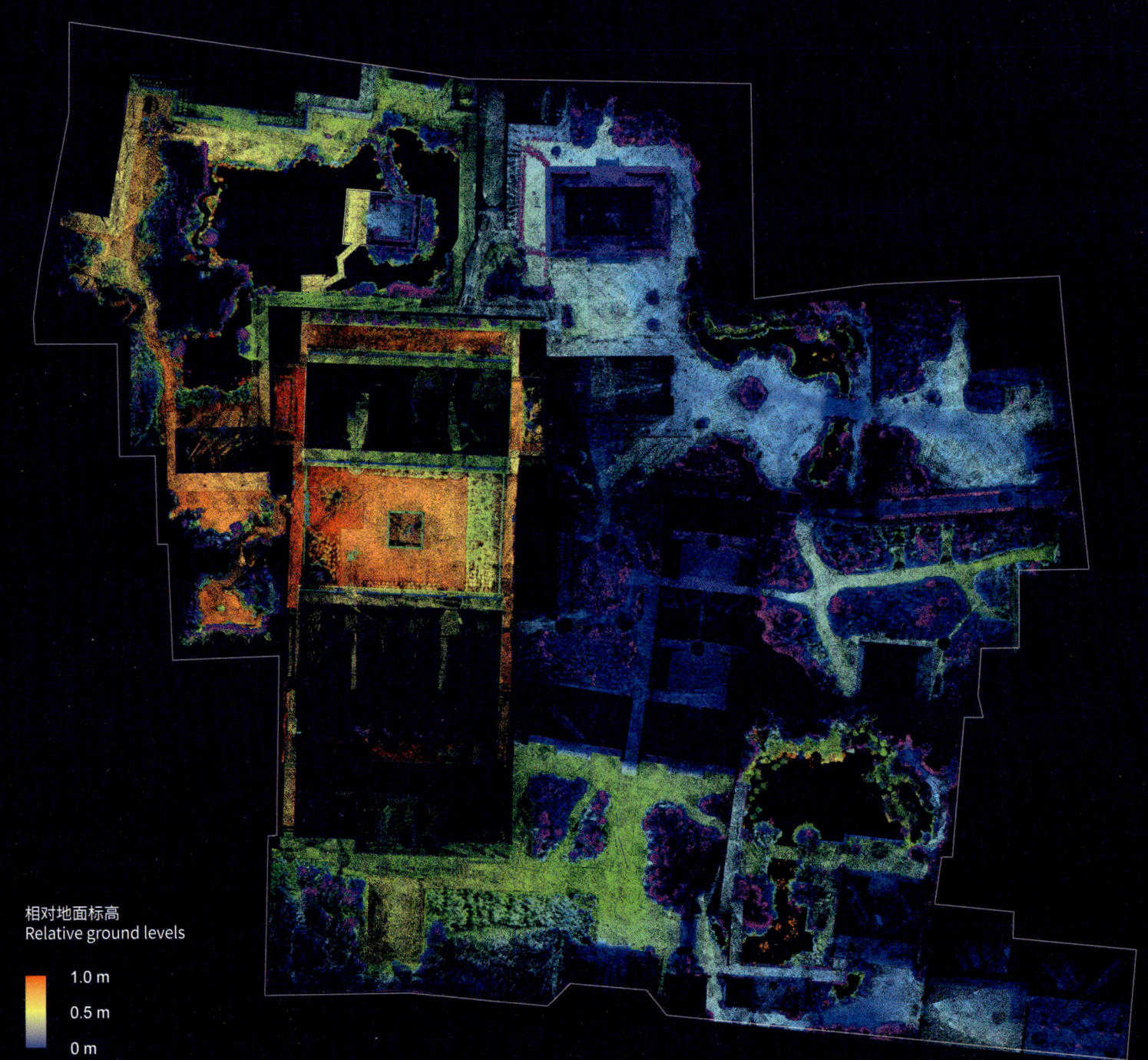

29 何园地面高程分析图
Relative ground levels of Heyuan Garden

相对地面标高
Relative ground levels

1.0 m
0.5 m
0 m

el Walkway. When Heyuan Garden was built, the owner designed a double-floored walkway to solve the problem of interconnecting different sections. The main buildings and yards were connected via the walkway. The walkway provides a semi-outdoor sheltered space for the residents during their daily movement around the complex. The walkway not only follows a complex route in plan, but changes in height. The complex spatial arrangement creates varied view lines and perspectives, creating a unique landscape experience. Walking along these pathways, the visitor seems to be in a Chinese scroll painting, with fascinating landscape images unfolding before them. The Double-Level Walkway itself also forms an important landscape interface. The cloister in the West Garden is two storeys high, encircling the pond, with varied railings and lattice windows creating a refined and elegant garden façade. The covered corridor is an important element in Chinese traditional gardens. Heyuan Garden inherits this tradition while at the same time innovating. The three-dimensional walking system centred on the Double-Level Walkway is unique in traditional Chinese private gardens and is an isolated example in Jiangnan gardens.

The combination of Chinese and Western styles for a people-oriented design

In the late Qing dynasty, with the increase of cultural exchange between China and Western countries, Yangzhou's gardens were also influenced by the West. He Weijian had once worked in customs and had experience dealing with foreigners. When he built Heyuan Garden, he introduced many Western elements and merged them with the qualities of traditional Chinese gardens to better satisfy living and recreation demands. These Western elements are mainly embodied in the buildings. For example, the use of Western-style elements such as blinds, fireplaces, and underground ventilation spaces improved the function of the Western-Style Building. New materials such as glass and metal railings were also introduced to Xuchun Hall (Cosy-Spring Hall) as decorations, which created a new building aesthetic. These characteristics may differ from traditional aesthetic standards of Chinese garden design, but this approach undoubtedly accurately reflected Chinese classical garden style as influenced by the West in the late Qing dynasty. From the perspective of garden development history, Heyuan Garden is a very precious example.

80
81

1

2

4

5

30 何园园林要素格局分析
Feature analysis of Heyuan Garden

1 假山
  Rockery
2 建筑
  Building
3 屋顶
  Roof
4 植物
  Vegetation
5 复道回廊
  Double-Level Walkway
6 水体
  Water

3

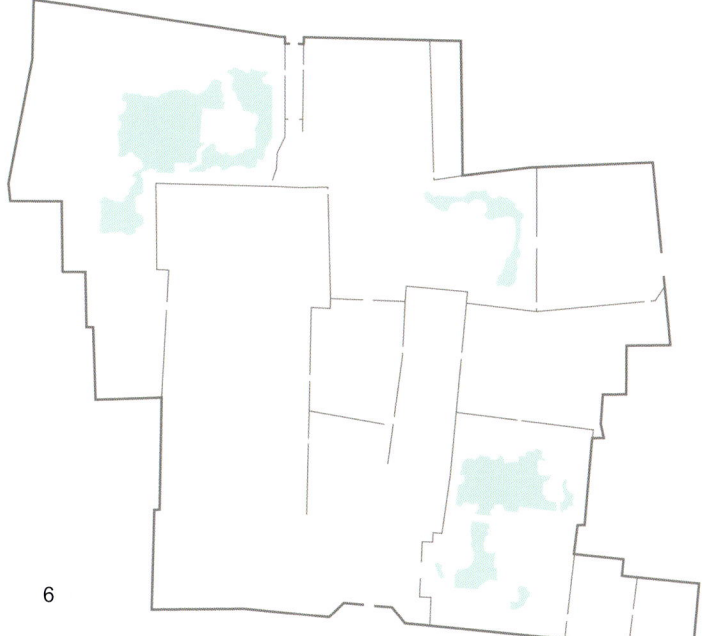

6

31 何园航拍图-c, 2019年6月
Aerial photo-c of Heyuan Garden, June 2019

08 园居院落
Residential Yards

32 园居院落轴测图
Isometric of the Residential Yards

图例 Legend

01 花园巷 Huayuan Lane
02 原南入口 Original South Entrance
03 与归堂 Yugui Hall
04 西洋楼 Western-Style Building
05 赏月楼 Shangyue Building (Moon-Viewing Building)
06 湖石假山 Taihu Lake stone rockery
07 骑马楼 Qima Building (Riding-Horse Building)
08 东一楼 First East Building
09 东二楼 Second East Building
10 东三楼 Third East Building
11 南门 South Entrance
12 女贞 *Ligustrum lucidum* Ait.
13 紫薇 *Lagerstroemia indica* L.
14 广玉兰 *Magnolia grandiflora* L.
15 木绣球 *Viburnum macrocephalum* Fort.

35 园居院落航拍图-a, 2019年6月
Aerial photo-a of the Residential Yards, June 2019

园居院落位于何园中部，是何氏家族生活起居的主要场所。院落分为东、西两条轴线，是以多组建筑围合而成的庭院空间。西部轴线的最南端是历史上何园在花园巷的南入口，现已不存。与归堂是当年人们进入何园之后看到的第一栋建筑，是接待宾客的正厅，从建筑和室外场地的尺度仍能感受到当年的气派。与归堂面阔七间，单檐歇山顶，整栋建筑都采用珍贵的楠木建造，是目前扬州市保存最好、面积最大的楠木厅之一。这栋建筑的门窗全部采用玻璃装饰，其中建筑大门两侧的两块玻璃足有4平方米，当年全部从国外进口，体现了园主雄厚的财力。

与归堂以北是一栋两进二层的住宅楼，是园主及家人的起居空间，当年被何家人称为"西洋楼"或"小洋楼"。西洋楼前后有通廊相连，楼间形成宽敞的院落。当年院子中央有两株对植的广玉兰，相传是从北美引进的树种，是清朝慈禧太后给有功官员的赏赐。20世纪50年代军管会入驻时，出于采光需要砍伐了东侧的一株，今日只有一株幸存，树龄已达130年。西洋楼的整体结构采用中国传统式的串楼样式，布局对称，其建筑的室内外装修引入了国外元素，例如法式的百叶门窗、壁炉和铁艺的床、日式的拉门等。西洋楼建造了两米高的地下室作为透气层，在接近地面处设计通风孔，很好地解决了建筑防潮的问题。20世纪90年代，著名画家李圣和先生以庭院内部的广玉兰和一株木绣球为灵感，将西洋楼起名为玉绣楼，此名一直沿用至今。

36 西洋楼内院，2019年6月
Courtyard of the Western-Style Building, June 2019

The Residential Yards are located in the middle of Heyuan Garden and are the main daily living spaces for the family. The precinct is arranged around two axes, one in the east and one in the west. The courtyards are enclosed by multiple building groups. The southernmost point of the western axis is the original entrance of Heyuan Garden into Huayuan Lane. This entry no longer exists. Historically Yugui Hall was the first building seen by people after entering the gardens. It was the main hall for guests. From the scale of the architecture and outdoor spaces, you can still feel the magnificence of old days. Yugui Hall is a seven-bay hall with a gable-and-hip roof. The entire building is built with the precious timber species, Phoebe nanmu, and is currently one of the best preserved and the largest traditional halls built with Phoebe nanmu in Yangzhou. The doors and windows of the building are all decorated with glass. The windows of glass on each side of the building's main entrance are four square metres in size. All are imported from abroad, reflecting the strong financial resources of the owner.

To the north of Yugui Hall is a two-storey building. It was the living space of the owner and his family. This building was called 'Xi Yang Lou' (Western-Style Building) or 'Xiao Yang Lou' (Little Foreign-Style Building) by the He family. There are corridors connecting the southern and northern buildings, and a spacious courtyard is formed between the two. At that time, there were two *Magnolia grandiflora* trees in the centre of the yard. It is said that these trees were introduced from North America. They were a gift from the Empress Dowager Cixi of the Qing dynasty to meritorious officials. When the military management committee was stationed in Heyuan Garden in the 1950s, one on the east side was cut down to improve natural lighting. Only one *Magnolia grandiflora* has survived until today, and is 130 years old. The overall structure of the Western-Style Building adopts the traditional Chinese style of string building with a symmetrical layout. The interior and exterior decoration of the building introduces foreign elements, such as French shutters and windows, fireplaces and wrought iron beds, Japanese-style sliding doors and so on. The Western-Style Building includes a two-metre-high basement as a ventilation layer incorporating vent holes at ground level, and solving the problem of building moisture. In the 1990s, the famous painter Li Shenghe was inspired by the *Magnolia grandiflora* ('Yulan' in Chinese) and an *Viburnum macrocephalum* ('Xiuqiu' in Chinese) in the courtyard. He named the building as Yuxiu Building and this name has been in use since then.

The east axis incorporates a group of buildings in the form of traditional Yangzhou houses. These buildings became the guest house of Heyuan Garden at that time. The southernmost part is a two storey, six-bay building. Because the shape of the building is like a saddle, and 'riding a horse' traditionally also meant 'travelling in foreign lands', the guest house is named Qima Building (Riding-Horse Building). Between the 10th year (1884) and the 20th year (1894) of the Guangxu reign in the Qing dynasty, Huang Binhong, a very famous Chinese painting master, visited Yangzhou 6 times. Huang is a relative of He Weijian, thus, he visited Heyuan Garden very often and lived in Qima Building. These visits started the communication of painting and calligraphy between Huang and He's family for more than 60 years. The east side of Qima Building, also known as the First East Building, extends northward to the Second East Building and the Third East Building, all in a form of Yangzhou local residential building with three main rooms, two wing-rooms and a court-

东路轴线是一组扬州传统民居形式的建筑，是当年何园的客舍。最南端的一栋面阔六间，进深七檩，单檐歇山顶，两层，分为东、西两幢。由于该楼的形状类似马鞍，"骑马"也意味着征途和异乡，因此称为"骑马楼"。清光绪十年（1884）至二十年（1894）间，中国著名国画大师黄宾虹曾六次到扬州，因他与园主人何维键有亲戚关系，故而是何园的常客，亦曾寓居于骑马楼，这开启了他与何家长达60余年的书画情缘。骑马楼靠东的一幢楼称为东一楼，依次向北延伸的两幢楼为东二楼和东三楼，均为上下三间两厢一天井的扬州民居楼形式，前后相连，两层上下相通，足够当年留宿客人之用。据考证，东部这组建筑保留了比较多的旧砖，有可能是光绪年间广东人吴辉谟在双槐园梅楼的旧址上修建的，何维键建造何园时略加修葺作为客舍使用。从测绘结果来看，这组建筑的轴线与片石山房及其南侧楠木厅（并非前文提及的与归堂）院落的轴线平行，但与寄啸山庄时期建设的西洋楼轴线有大约5°的夹角。由此可以推断片石山房与东路轴线上这组建筑很可能是同一时期或同一个住宅内的建构。

在西洋楼的西侧，另外有一处僻静的院落和一栋两层小楼，名曰赏月楼，又可称怡萱楼，是当年何维键为其母亲建造的居所。赏月楼坐北朝南，面阔三间，楼南有一座小院，院中有一座太湖石假山，假山二层与建筑二层以蹬道相连，山下有山洞、石阶可以穿行。赏月楼以健康长寿、贞操德行为主题，建筑走廊的栏杆上有延年益寿字样的图案，楼前地面也用卵石铺成福禄寿喜图案。院落中种植松柏象征长寿、女贞象征节操、紫薇象征和睦、石榴象征多子，许多株树木都有130年以上的树龄，为当年何园初建时栽植，其中东部院门前的女贞树据说是何母亲手栽植的。

yard. The buildings are connected to each other, and the two floors are also connected. According to investigation, this group of buildings in the east retains a lot of old bricks. It was likely built by Wu Huimo from Gurangdong in the Guangxu reign on the site of Meilou Building in Twin Pagoda Trees Garden. When Heyuan Garden was built in 1883, He Weijian repaired it and used it as a guest house. From the results of the survey, the axis of this building group is parallel to the axis of the Small-Rock Mountain Retreat and the Phoebe nanmu Hall (not the above-mentioned Yugui Hall) courtyard in the south, but it has an angle of about 5° with the axis of the Western-Style Building constructed by the He's family. From this it can be inferred that the buildings on the axis of the Small-Rock Mountain Retreat and the East axis are likely to be constructed in the same period or in the same residence.

On the west side of the Western-Style Building, there is another secluded courtyard and a two-storey building. The building is called Shangyue Building (Moon-Viewing Building), also known as Yixuan Building. It was built by He Weijian for his mother. Shangyue Building faces south. It is three-bays wide with a small courtyard to the south. There is an artificial mountain made from Taihu Lake stone in the courtyard. The upper level of the rockery is connected with the second floor of the building. There are caves and stone steps under the mountain. The theme of Shangyue Building is health, longevity and chastity. The railings of the building's upper level verandah incorporate a pattern representing longevity. The ground in front of the building is paved with pebbles. The planting of pine and cypress trees in the courtyard also symbolises longevity, the *Ligustrum lucidum* tree symbolises chastity, *Lagerstroemia indica* symbolises harmony, and *Punica granatum* (pomegranate) implies fertility. Many of these trees have an age of more than 130 years. They were planted when Heyuan Garden was first built. The *Ligustrum lucidum* in front of the eastern courtyard is said to be planted by He's mother.

37 何园西部整体剖面图
The overall section of the western part of Heyuan Garden

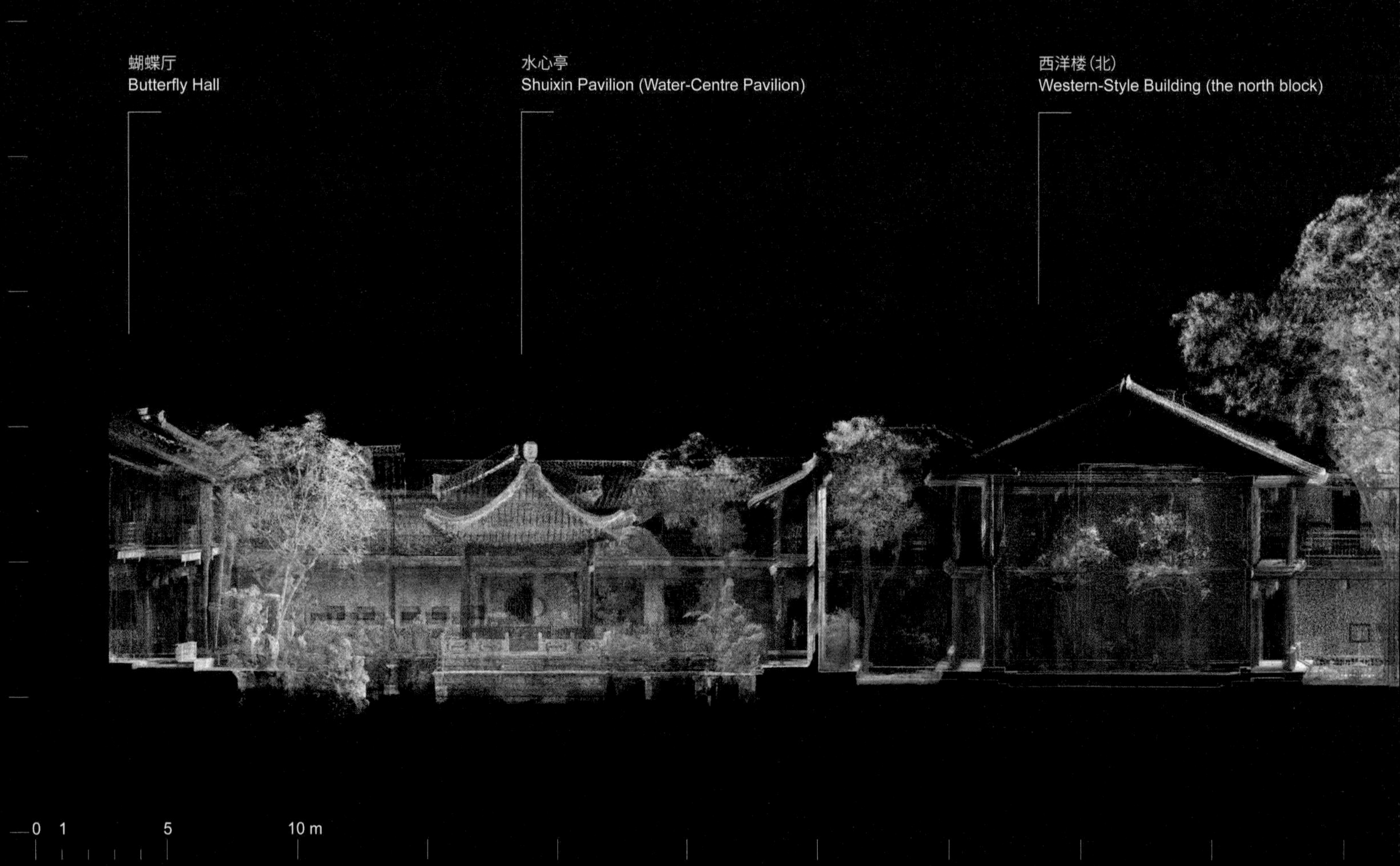

蝴蝶厅
Butterfly Hall

水心亭
Shuixin Pavilion (Water-Centre Pavilion)

西洋楼（北）
Western-Style Building (the north block)

0 1   5   10 m

广玉兰
Magnolia grandiflora L.

西洋楼（南）
Western-Style Building (the south block)

与归堂
Yugui Hall

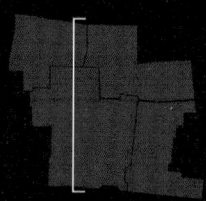

38 何园中部整体剖面图
The overall section of the middle part of Heyuan Garden

近月亭
Jinyue Pavilion (Moon-Approaching Pavilion)

贴壁假山
Wall rockery

牡丹厅
Mudan Hall (Peony Hall)

东三楼
Third East Building

0 1   5   10 m

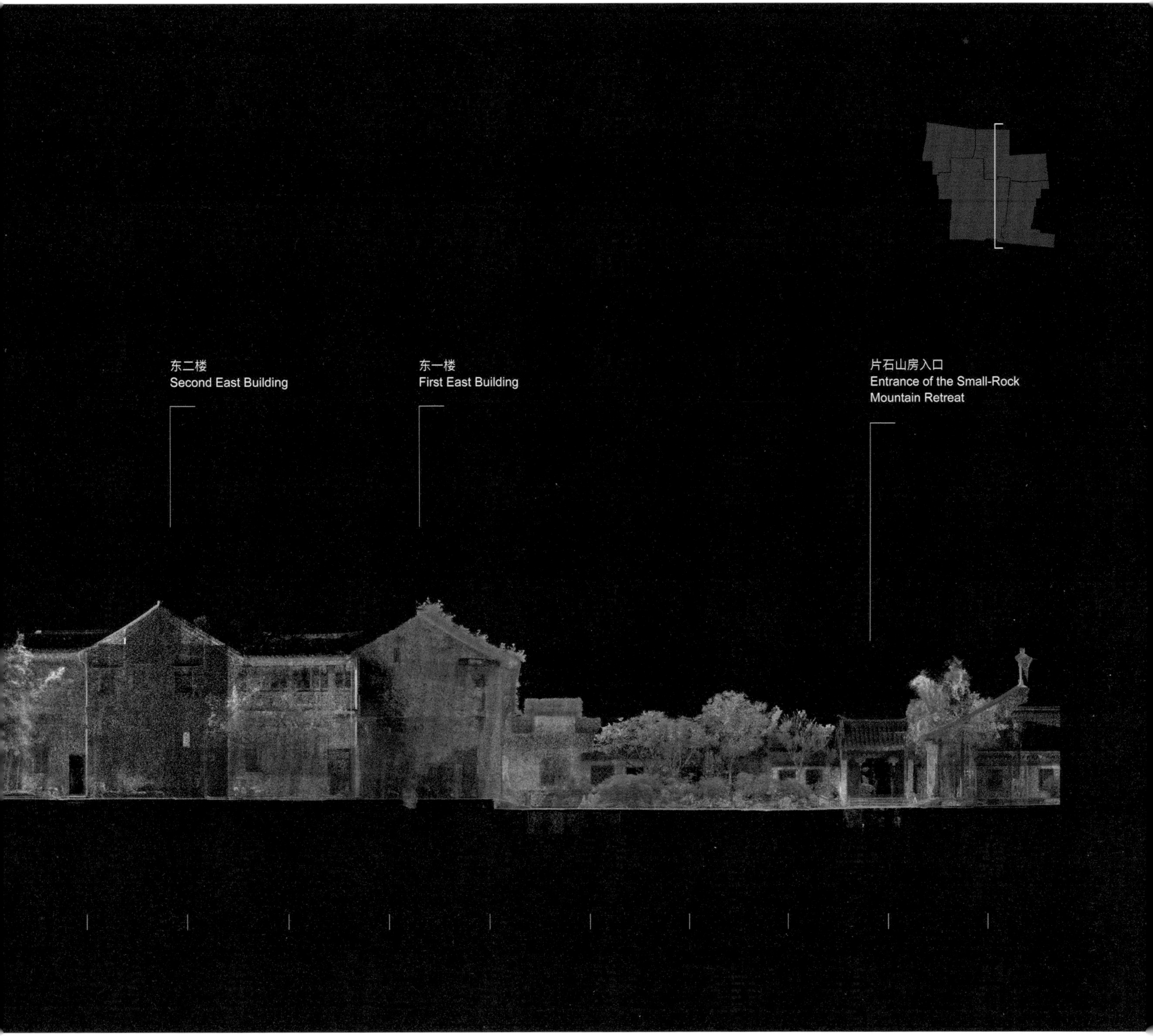

东二楼
Second East Building

东一楼
First East Building

片石山房入口
Entrance of the Small-Rock Mountain Retreat

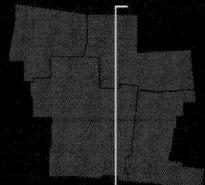

39 与归堂立面图
Elevation of Yugui Hall

40 骑马楼立面图
Elevation of Qima Building

41 园居院落航拍图-b，2018年12月
Aerial photo-b of the Residential Yards, December 2018

42 赏月楼与西洋楼立面图
Elevation of Shangyue Building and the Western-Style Building

43 赏月楼立面，2019年6月
Shangyue Building, June 2019

44 西洋楼北部立面图
North elevation of the Western-Style Building

45 西洋楼南部立面图
South elevation of the Western-Style Building

46 西洋楼西部立面图
West elevation of the Western-Style Building

47 西洋楼东部立面图
East elevation of the Western-Style Building

48 何维键的曾(外)孙女何祚惠(左)和王承礼在西洋楼合影, 1935年. 来源:扬州何园管理处提供
He Zuohui (left) and Wang Chengli, the great-granddaughters of He Weijian in front of the Western-Style Building, 1935. Source: Management Office of Heyuan Garden, Yangzhou

49 西洋楼外廊，2019年6月
The veranda of the Western-Style Building, June 2019

50 赏月楼院落剖面图-a
Section-a of Shangyue Building yard

赏月楼
Shangyue Building (Moon-Viewing Building)

女贞
Ligustrum lucidum Ait.

51 赏月楼院落剖面图-b
Section-b of Shangyue Building yard

太湖石假山
Taihu Lake stone rockery

赏月楼
Shangyue Building (Moon-Viewing Building)

09 西园
West Garden

52 西园轴测图
Isometric of the West Garden

53 西园点云正射影像图
   Orthographic point cloud map of the West Garden

54 西园一层平面图
   Ground floor plan of the West Garden

55 西园航拍图, 2019年6月
Aerial photo of the West Garden, June 2019

园居院落以北是何园的花园部分，分东、西两个院落，是当年园主精心营造的园林空间，被称为"寄啸山庄"（寄啸山庄亦可指整座何园），何家人称之"大花园"，与东南部的"小花园"（片石山房）遥相呼应。西园是何园最重要的花园，是当年园主招待宾客、雅集宴饮的主要空间。花园北侧的刁家巷有一处单独的园门，砖雕门楼上有主人何维键亲笔题写的隶书"寄啸山庄"门额，宾客当年可由此门直接进入花园。

西园以矩形水池为中心，池西堆叠了一座大型假山，假山以太湖石为主峰。靠近西侧园墙的部分由黄石堆叠，这在中国传统园林叠山中并不多见，据说是20世纪60年代无线电厂驻用何园期间破坏了原有太湖石假山后修补的结果。假山主峰高耸，山上有石磴道盘旋而上可以登临峰顶。两株白皮松高大挺拔，已有130余年的树龄，凸显了假山的高耸之势。正对假山景观的是水池中央的水心亭。水亭在中国传统园林中有"小方壶"之美称（"方壶"是神话传说中一座海上仙山的名字）。水心亭单檐，四方攒尖顶，装饰精美典雅，亭下建白石平台，平台外侧构白石望柱和栏杆。亭南有曲桥与池岸相连，亭北有太湖石桥与岸相接，将水池分隔成为大小两个水域空间，给人以连绵不尽的感觉。

水池北侧是园林的主体建筑，高两层，面宽七楹，中部主楼三间略高，因形若蝴蝶，故称作蝴蝶厅，也叫七间厅。蝴蝶厅一层是园主会客宴请的主要场所，因此也称作宴厅；二层是何家的藏书楼，原名梅花阁，现又称为汇胜楼，主人当年于此收藏古今典籍、名家字画。根据测绘结果，蝴蝶厅南北向轴线与东一楼、东二楼、东三楼以及片石山房院落轴线基本一致，很可能是同一时期或同一宅园遗留下来的特征。西园的西北角为桂花厅，坐西朝东，面阔三间，掩映于山石、桂树丛中，为清幽的赏桂之处。

西园水池南侧则是复道回廊的主体部分。何园内的复道回廊连通上下，贯穿全园。廊道随地赋形，变化丰富，根据位置和景观的不同，有双层双面廊、双层单面廊、单层单面廊等不同形式。其中部分廊段为复廊，即在双面廊中间设一道隔墙，将长廊分成两个步道，并在隔墙上设置漏窗、书法石刻等装饰，形成半室内的空间。复道回廊向东连通东园的读书楼，向南延伸到园居院落的西洋楼、骑马楼，形成了便捷的交通空间。复道回廊也用于分隔景区，并通过墙上的漏窗提供视线联系，增加景观的层次性。廊的高低、曲折变化也在引导着观赏园林的视点和视线，提供了俯视园林的视角，丰富了园林的体验。在西园中，复道回廊三面环抱水景，构成了静谧典雅的园林界面，是何园中最美的风景之一。

To the north of the residential area is the major garden carefully created by He Weijian. It is called 'Jixiao Shanzhuang' (Whistling Scholar's Mountain Retreat) and the name also refers to the whole Heyuan Garden complex. The He Family used to call it 'Large Garden', and the southeastern garden 'Little Garden' (Small-Rock Mountain Retreat). The major garden precinct is divided into two courtyards, the East Garden and the West Garden. The West Garden is the most important space of Heyuan Garden. It was the main gathering venue for the He family and their guests. There is an individual gateway on the north side of the garden. On the gateway, made from bricks of fine clay, there is a gate plaque from the owner, He Weijian, who wrote the name 'Jixiao Shanzhuang'. In that period, the guests could enter the garden directly through this backdoor.

The West Garden is centred on a rectangular pond. To the west of the pond, there is a large rockery, of which the peak is predominantly made of Taihu Lake stone. The part near the west wall is stacked yellow stones. It is rare in traditional Chinese gardens to use two types of stone in one rockery. It is said that this is the result of damage to the original Taihu Lake stone rockery and the repairs that followed when the radio factory was located here in the 20th century. The main peak of the rockery is towering, and there are stone winding roads that climb to the summit. Two white bark pines are tall and straight highlighting the height of the rockery and are more than 130 years old. Facing the rockery landscape, in the centre of the pond, is a water pavilion named Shuixin Pavilion (Water-Centre Pavilion). Water pavilions can be called 'Xiao Fanghu' (the small square pot) in traditional Chinese gardens as 'Fanghu' is said to be one of the mountain homes for the immortals in Chinese mythology. Shuixin pavilion has a single pyramidal tent shape roof with a decorative cap at the apex. The pavilion is exquisitely decorated and elegant, on top of a white stone platform and with white stone pillars and railings arranged around the perimeter. There are two bridges; one on the south and one on the north connecting the pavilion to the surrounding land area. The pond is divided into two water surfaces by the bridges, giving visitors a sense of endlessness.

On the north side of the pond is the main building of the West Garden. It is two storeys high and seven bays wide. To the north of the large pond in the centre of the garden sits a seven-span hall. The three central spans protrude slightly and two roof wings extend sideways with upturned eaves. As the entire building looks like a flying butterfly, locals call it the Butterfly Hall ('Hudie Ting' in Chinese). The first floor of the Butterfly Hall is the main place for banquets, and consequently is also called the Banquet Hall. The second floor houses the family library, also known as Meihua Belvedere (Plum-Blossom Belvedere) or Huisheng Building. This is where the owner collected ancient books, famous calligraphy and paintings. The survey shows that the north-south axis of the Butterfly Hall is on the same alignment as that of the First East Building, the Second East Building, the Third East Building, and the Small-Rock Mountain Retreat. These various elements were probably constructed at the same time and might also be part of a single property. In the northwest corner of the West Garden is the Guihua Hall (Osmanthus Hall), three bays wide and facing east. It is a quiet and elegant yard for admiring the *Osmanthus*.

The main part of the Double-Level Walkway is located on the south side of the West Garden pond. The Double-Level Walkway in Heyuan Garden is

56 西园透视图
Perspective of the West Garden

designed relative to its context, location and surrounding landscape, linking the upper and lower levels to connect the whole garden. The walkway assumes a variety of forms: in some sections there are two-sided corridors on the both floors; elsewhere there might be single-sided ones upstairs and/or downstairs. The sections in two-sided form sometimes set a wall to separate the corridor into two passageways. The walls are covered with leaking windows and calligraphy stone carvings to form a semi-indoor space. The Double-Level Walkway forms a convenient passageway system from the Reading Building ('Dushu Lou' in Chinese) in the East Garden to the Western-Style Building and Qima Building (Riding-Horse Building) in the Residential Yards. The passageways are also used to separate the various scenic spots and often provide visual connections through the framed window wall openings multiplying the layers of landscape. The change of height and shape of the corridor also guide the visitor to viewing points and sights of the garden. They provide new perspectives overlooking the garden and enriching the landscape experience. In the West Garden, the pond is wrapped by the Double-Level Walkway on three sides, creating a quiet and elegant garden interface. This creates some of the most beautiful scenery in Heyuan Garden.

57 水心亭，摄于1983年. 来源：陈从周,《扬州园林》，上海：同济大学出版社, 2007

Shuixin Pavilion, 1983. Source: Chen Congzhou, *Yangzhou Gardens*, Shanghai: Tongji University Press, 2007

120
121

58 西园底层轴测图
West Garden lower level isometric

122
123

59 西园上层轴测图
West Garden upper level isometric

60 蝴蝶厅立面图
Elevation of the Butterfly Hall

61 蝴蝶厅,摄于1983年. 来源:陈从周,《扬州园林》,
上海:同济大学出版社,2007

The Butterfly Hall, 1983. Source: Chen Congzhou, *Yangzhou Gardens*. Shanghai: Tongji University Press, 2007

对比1983年的照片,蝴蝶厅和周围的水池、驳岸,以及西侧的太湖石假山并未出现明显变化。

The characteristics of the Butterfly Hall and the surrounding pond, revetment, and the Taihu Lake stone rockery on the western side have not changed significantly since the 1983 photograph.

62 蝴蝶厅, 2019年6月
The Butterfly Hall, June 2019

63 西园剖面图
Section of the West Garden

复道回廊
Double-Level Walkway

64 复道回廊内景,2018年6月
Interior of the Double-Level Walkway, June 2018

65 复道回廊,摄于1983年. 来源:陈从周,《扬州园林》,上海:同济大学出版社,2007

The Double-Level Walkway, 1983. Source: Chen Congzhou, *Yangzhou Gardens*, Shanghai: Tongji University Press, 2007

66 复道回廊，2019年6月
The Double-Level Walkway, June 2019

67 西园南部剖面图
Section of the southern part of the West Garden

白皮松
Pinus bungeana Zucc. ex Endl.

0 1   5   10 m

68 西园水心亭剖面图
Section of Shuixin Pavilion in the West Garden

69 西园复道回廊立面图-a
Elevation-a of the Double-Level Walkway in the West Garden

70 西园复道回廊立面图-b
Elevation-b of the Double-Level Walkway in the West Garden

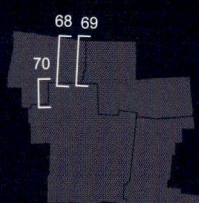

石楠
Photinia serrulata Lindl.

71 西园假山剖面图
Section of the rockery in the West Garden

72 西园湖石假山主峰，2019年6月
The peak of the rockery in the West Garden, June 2019

73 西园假山与复道回廊，2019年6月
The rockery and the Double-Level Walkway in the West Garden, June 2019

74 西园假山与复道回廊, 摄于1983年. 来源: 陈从周,《扬州园林》,
上海: 同济大学出版社, 2007
The rockery and the Double-Level Walkway in the West Garden, 1983.
Source: Chen Congzhou, *Yangzhou Gardens*, Shanghai: Tongji University Press, 2007

75 西园水池与水心亭，摄于1983年. 来源：陈从周，《扬州园林》. 上海：同济大学出版社，2007

The pond and Shuixin Pavilion in the West Garden, 1983. Source: Chen Congzhou, *Yangzhou Gardens*. Shanghai: Tongji University Press, 2007.

76 西园水池与水心亭，2019年6月

The pond and Shuixin Pavilion in the West Garden, June 2019

77 水心亭透视图
Perspective of Shuixin Pavilion

78 水心亭立面图
Elevations of Shuixin Pavilion

10 东园
East Garden

79 东园轴测图
Isometric of the East Garden

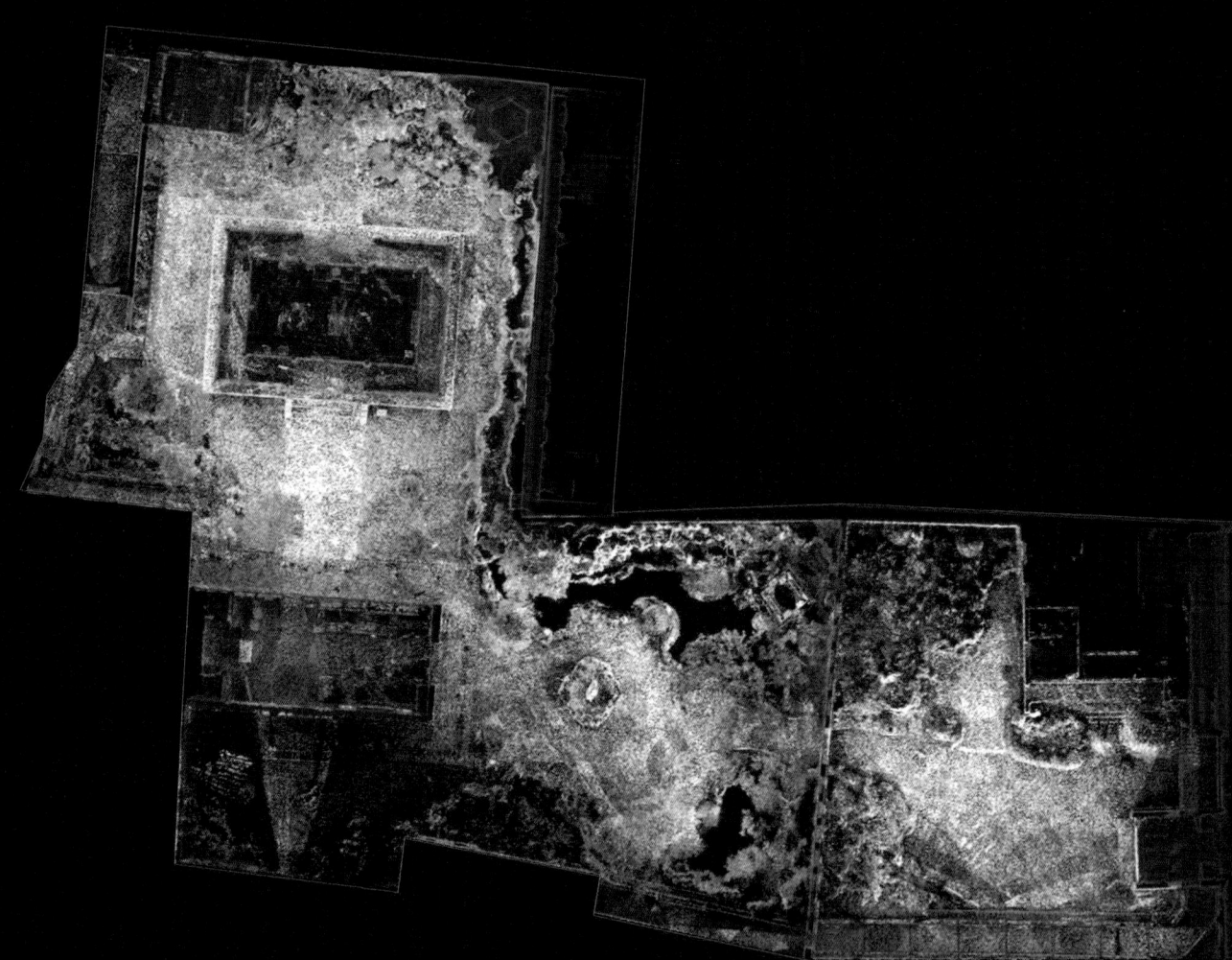

图例 Legend	01 桴海轩（船厅）Fuhai Hall (the Boat Hall)	06 接风亭 Jiefeng Pavilion (Wind-Embracing Pavilion)	12 瓜子黄杨 *Buxus microphylla* Sieb. et Zucc
	02 牡丹厅 Mudan Hall (Peony Hall)	07 东门 East Entrance	13 瓜子黄杨 *Buxus microphylla* Sieb. et Zucc
	03 读书楼 Reading Building	08 徐凝门大街 Xuningmen Street	14 桂花 *Osmanthus fragrans* (Thunb.) Lour.
	04 贴壁假山 Wall Rockery	09 办公用房 Office building	15 桂花 *Osmanthus fragrans* (Thunb.) Lour.
	05 近月亭 Jinyue Pavilion (Moon-Approaching Pavilion)	10 游客中心 Tourist Centre	16 黄杨 *Buxus sinica* (Rehd. et Wils.) Cheng
		11 丝棉木 *Euonymus maackii* Rupr.	

82 东园航拍图-a, 2019年6月
Aerial photo-a of the East Garden, June 2019

与西园相比，东园是一座以建筑为主体的院落。主体建筑桴海轩位于东园西北部，是当年园主待茶之所。桴海轩为单檐歇山式建筑，四周有回廊，厅似船形，四周以鹅卵石、瓦片铺地，形成水波状图案，是扬州古典园林中独特的"旱园水作"手法，因此该建筑又称作"船厅"。园主何维键的官职和水运、船只相关，因此辞官隐居后借用船的形象隐喻宦海沉浮。船厅前有一对楹联："月作主人梅作客，花为四壁船为家"，更是点明了此景的意境。吴氏双槐园的两棵古槐树直到20世纪60年代以前还存在于船厅南侧，曾与船厅相映成趣。

船厅西侧走廊的墙壁上有一处重要的文物，即《海市（并叙）》石刻。《海市（并叙）》是中国宋代杰出的诗文大家苏轼的作品，主要描写海市蜃楼的海上神山仙境。何维键建造何园时，将这部书法作品做成石刻置于园林墙壁之上，以此表达其寄情自然的造园初衷，也说明其造园时即以"海上仙山"为所求意境。船厅以南是东园内另外一栋主体建筑牡丹厅，该建筑坐北朝南，面阔三间，进深七檩，因其东面歇山嵌有"凤吹牡丹"砖雕而得名。该砖雕是扬州晚清时期的精品，在20世纪50年代从古城区另一处园林内迁建至此。

在东园的北部院墙上有一处长约65米的贴壁假山，以太湖石堆叠，参差蜿蜒，连绵不断。此山是中国传统园林假山中独具特色的峭壁山，也称为贴壁假山、壁岩。假山倚墙而筑，以粉墙为纸，山石为墨，形成山水画意境。这座假山从东部二道门的接风亭起，沿园墙西行，与船厅西北角上的半月台相接，并一直向西与读书楼的二层相连。假山下有石洞，中有洞室，上有蹬道，形成完整的连续画面。贴壁假山减弱了园林围墙的人工感，同时倚靠园墙堆叠，也节省了空间和石材，是扬派叠石的典型代表。

东园以东是1986年补建在徐凝门大街上的新入口，也是今天游客进入何园的主要入口和集散空间。测绘发现东侧入口处有两段高度一致但不相连的高墙，或许标示着何园历史上的范围和园墙位置。

Compared with the West Garden, the East Garden is a courtyard dominated by buildings. The main building named Fuhai Hall, a pavilion with windows on four sides, is in the northwest of the East Garden. Fuhai Hall was a tearoom for the family guests. It has a gable-and-hip roof, with corridors on four sides. The hall itself is like a boat, which is surrounded by pebbles and tiles forming a water-wave pattern. This is a typical gardening method in Yangzhou called 'hanyuan shuizuo' (a water-less garden is made to look like water-bound), which uses pavement texture changes to form an imaginary water landscape with little or no water. Therefore, Fuhai Hall is also known as the Ship Hall ('Chuan Ting' in Chinese). The official position of the owner, He Weijian, was related to water transport and ships, therefore, after his resignation, the image of a ship was used to metaphorically represent the rise and fall of his career. In front of the Ship Hall, there is a couplet hung on the columns: 'The moon is the host and the plum blossom is the guest, the flowers form the walls and the ship is home.' The poem alludes to the artistic conception of this place. The two ancient pagoda trees of the Wu's Garden existed on the south side of the Ship Hall until the 1960s once forming a delightful contrast with the building.

There is another important cultural relic on the wall of the corridor, namely the 'Mirage' stone inscription. 'Mirage' is the writing of Su Shi, one of the most accomplished figures in classical Chinese literature. 'Mirage' mainly depicts the immortals and the wonderland at sea imagined by the author. When He Weijian built Heyuan Garden, he inscribed this calligraphy work on the wall to express his original intention of gardening, and built the garden with the 'fairy mountain at sea' as the artistic conception. To the south of the Ship Hall is another main building, Mudan Hall (Peony Hall). The building historically faced south and is three bays wide. It is named after the phoenix and peony brick carving embedded in the east gable. The brick carving is an exquisite work of carving from the late Qing dynasty in Yangzhou. The brick carving was relocated from another garden in the historic town of Yangzhou in the 1950s.

In the northern part of the East Garden there is a 65-metre-long artificial mountain pushed against the garden's boundary walls. The Taihu Lake stone rockery is stacked, staggering and continuous along the walls. This 'mountain' is a unique cliff mountain in the traditional Chinese garden rockery. This type of design is called a wall rockery. The rockery is built against a wall, where the wall is used as drawing paper, and the painting is made of stones. This rockery starts from Jiefeng Pavilion (Wind-Embracing Pavilion) in the east and runs west along the wall. It is connected to the half-moon-shaped platform on the northwest corner of the Ship Hall and is connected to the second floor of the Reading Building to the west. There are stone stairways and caves under the rockery, and there are ramps on the hills to form a complete continuous terrain. The mountain range hides the wall and diminishes the sense that the garden is an artificially enclosed space. At the same time the technique saves space and stone and is typically representative of Yangzhou rockery construction.

On the eastern side of the East Garden is a new yard and entrance built in 1986 connecting Heyuan Garden to Xuningmen Street. Today it is the main entrance and distribution space for visitors. The survey work shows that the east side entrance has high walls with the same height but not connected at both ends, indicating the original range of the garden and the position of the garden wall.

83 东园航拍图-b, 2019年6月
Aerial photo-b of the East Garden, June 2019

84 东园贴壁假山轴测图
East Garden wall rockery isometric

近月亭
Jinyue Pavilion (Moon-Approaching Pavilion)

85 东园贴壁假山立面图（东段）
East Garden wall rockery elevation (east section)

接风亭
Jiefeng Pavilion (Wind-Embracing Pavilion)

East Garden wall rockery elevation (west section)

读书楼
Reading Building

87 东园贴壁假山立面图（中段）
East Garden wall rockery elevation (middle section)

贴壁假山
Wall rockery

接风亭
Jiefeng Pavilion (Wind-Embracing Pavilion)

88（左）近月亭，摄于1983年. 来源：陈从周，《扬州园林》，上海：同济大学出版社，2007

(left) Jinyue Pavilion, 1983. Source: Chen Congzhou, *Yangzhou Gardens*, Shanghai: Tongji University Press, 2007

89（右）近月亭，2018年12月
(right) Jinyue Pavilion, December 2018

从历史照片来看，近月亭上的宝顶由原来的球形变成现在的六边形，假山上原有一株朴树，现仅存树根。

The historical photo shows that the top of Jinyue Pavilion (Moon-Appoaching Pavilion) has changed from the original spherical shape to the current hexagon. There was a hackberry tree (*Celtis sinensis*) on the rockery, but only the stump remains today.

90. 东园航拍图-c, 2019年6月
Aerial photo-c of the East Garden, June 2019

接风亭
Jiefeng Pavilion (Wind-Embracing Pavilion)

黄杨
Buxus sinica (Rehd. et Wils.) Cheng

91 东园东院立面图
Elevation of the east yard of the East Garden

丝棉木
Euonymus maackii Rupr.

游客中心
Tourist Centre

92 东园东院云墙立面图
Section of the cloud-shaped wall in the east yard of the East Garden

93　东园门，摄于1984年. 来源：朱江，《扬州园林品赏录》，
上海：上海文化出版社，1984
Gate of the East Garden, 1984. Source: Zhu Jiang, *Appreciation of Yangzhou Gardens*, Shanghai: Shanghai Culture Press, 1984

94　东园门，2019年6月
Gate of the East Garden, June 2019

95 樟海轩前的石峰和槐树，2019年6月
The rock and pagoda tree in front of Fuhai Hall, June 2019

96 桴海轩前的石峰和槐树,摄于1983年. 来源:陈从周,《扬州园林》,上海:同济大学出版社,2007

The rock and pagoda tree in front of Fuhai Hall, 1983. Source: Chen Congzhou, *Yangzhou Gardens*, Shanghai: Tongji University Press, 2007

97 桴海轩（船厅），摄于1983年．来源：陈从周，《扬州园林》，上海：同济大学出版社，2007
Fuhai Hall (the Boat Hall), 1983. Source: Chen Congzhou, *Yangzhou Gardens*, Shanghai: Tongji University Press, 2007

98 桴海轩（船厅），2019年6月
Fuhai Hall (the Boat Hall), June 2019

99 牡丹厅东山墙上的"凤吹牡丹"砖雕，2019年6月
The phoenix and peony brick carving embedded in the east gable of Mudan Hall, June 2019

11 片石山房及其他区域
Small-Rock Mountain Retreat and Other Precincts

注：示意图仅标出片石山房区域。
Note: Only the Small-Rock Mountain Retreat precinct is illustrated here.

100 片石山房轴测图
Isometric of the Small-Rock Mountain Retreat

101 片石山房点云正射影像图
Orthographic point cloud map of the Small-Rock Mountain Retreat

102 片石山房一层平面图
Ground floor plan of the Small-Rock Mountain Retreat

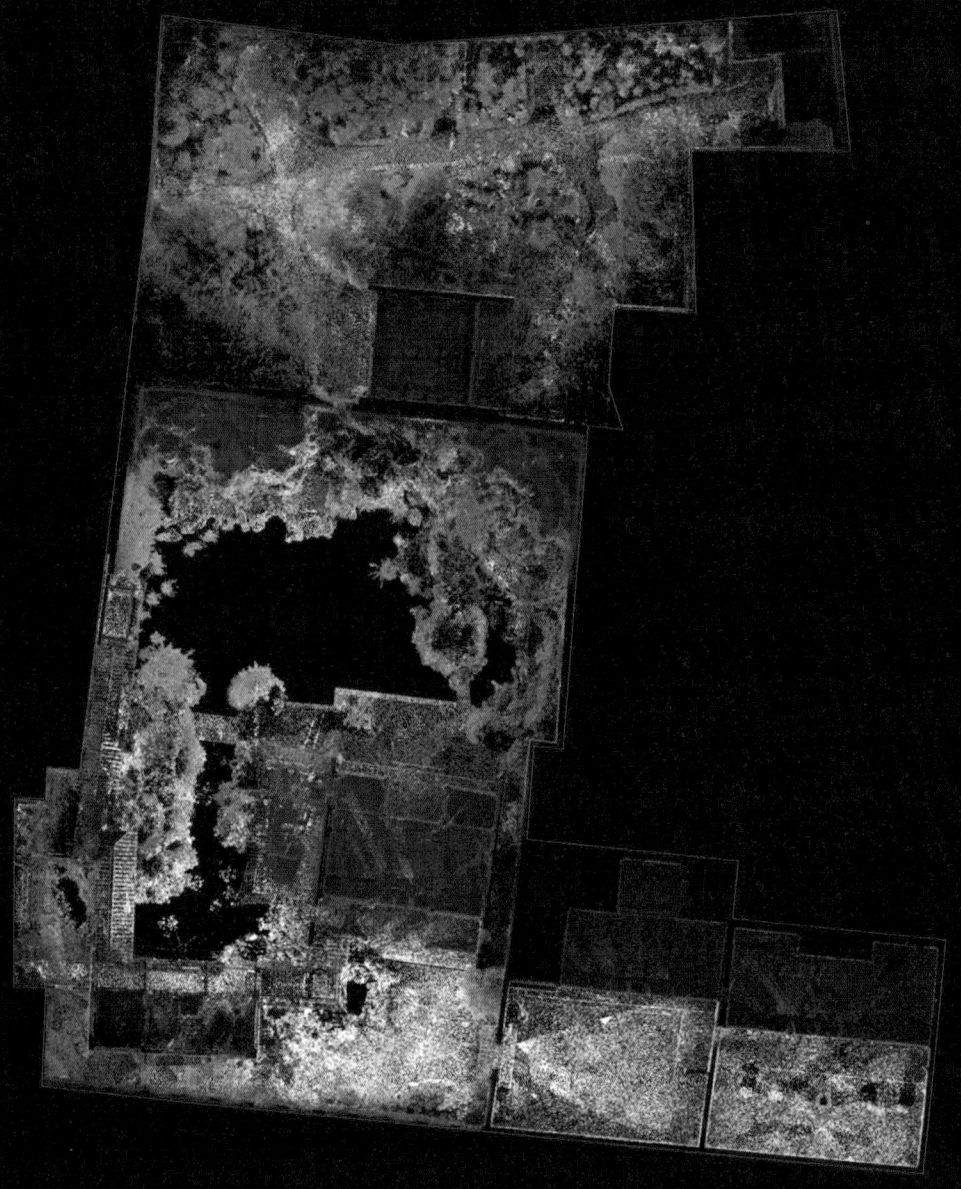

103 片石山房航拍图, 2019年6月
Aerial photo of the Small-Rock Mountain Retreat, June 2019

片石山房位于何园的东南角，是一个独立的院落，其主景是倚靠北部院墙的一座太湖石假山。据考证，这座假山的创作者是清代著名山水画家、扬州画派的先驱石涛。假山平面呈横长形，西部为主峰，根据测绘结果，主峰高8.75米，特立耸秀，奇峭迎人。主峰下有两间方形石室，即所谓"片石山房"。假山以小块太湖石拼镶而成，利用石块大小组合以及纹理横直组成峰峦，并按照绘画理论进行营构。假山布局紧凑、手法统一，体量虽大但没有一点人工的痕迹，显示出极高的艺术水平和叠山技巧。假山东部有一株300年树龄的小叶罗汉松，可旁证假山的古老年代。假山南部为水池，池南为楠木厅，据考证很可能是清代双槐园遗构，也是何园内最为古老的木构建筑。

1962年，古建园林专家陈从周先生发现这座假山时，仅存西侧的主峰和东侧石洞，中间部分假山已经倾倒，无法看到其原貌。1989年，古典园林专家吴肇钊和叠山名师孙玉根修复了片石山房假山，修复方案对遗存部分进行了充分保护和妥善利用，并以石涛的画稿为蓝本，参考何家人对片石山房假山的回忆，将东西两段假山连接起来，并以水池考古边界为依据，将方池恢复成为曲池，还修复了东南侧的楠木厅。同时，在假山南端增建了硬山水榭三间，东部建曲廊与楠木厅相接，并于厅西山墙建造歇山舫屋，从而形成完整的庭院空间。

片石山房以东是何家祠堂，原先为何家供奉祖先牌位的地方。现存何家祠堂是一座两层的主楼和十多间砖木结构的平房。祠堂内东西呈一字排开的两座厅堂，各自有独立的院落。西部为享堂，堂西有一座厢房，原为签押房，管理何家各种往来的项目。东部为寝堂，是祠堂的正厅，供有保存完好的何氏祖宗容像。

Located on the southeast corner of Heyuan Garden, the Small-Rock Mountain Retreat is an independent courtyard. The main landscape is an artificial Taihu Lake stone rockery leaning against the northern wall. According to research, the author of this rockery is Shitao, a famous painter of the Qing dynasty and pioneer of the Yangzhou School of Painting. The mountain faces south, and, judging from its plane, it is a wall-leaning rock formation with its width exceeding its height. The main peak should have stood at its western end, with its steep and verdant form rising in the wind, nodding its fantastic head at the visitor while looking down upon a pond at its foot. According to the results of this survey, the main peak is 8.75 metres high. There are two square rooms built of bricks below the mountain, which is why the entire rockwork is called Small-Rock Mountain Retreat ('Pianshi Shanfang' in Chinese). The rockery is made up of small pieces of Taihu Lake stone, and its ridges and peaks are composed of combinations of varying stone sizes and textures and are constructed according to the theory of painting. The rockery layout is compact and uniform. While the volume is large, there is no trace of artificiality, showing a very high artistic level and stacking skills. In the eastern part of the rockery, there is a 300-year-old lobular yacca (*Podocarpus macrophyllus*), marking the ancient age of the rockery. There is a three-framed Phoebe nanmu hall remains on the southern side of the pond. According to the research, it should have been built during the Qianlong reign of the Qing dynasty. It is probably the remains of Wu's Twin Pagoda Trees Garden.

When classical garden master Chen Congzhou discovered this rockery in 1962, only the main peak on the west side and the stone cave on the east side existed. The middle part of the rockery had been destroyed and could not be seen. In 1989, Wu Zhaozhao, a classical garden expert, and Sun Yugen, a rockery master, repaired the artificial mountain. The restoration plan fully protected and utilised the remains and learned from Shitao's paintings and the records from the He family. The two sections of the rockery are connected with new sympathetic elements. Based on the archaeological survey of the pond, the square pond has been restored into a curved pond, and the Phoebe nanmu Hall on the southeast side was restored. At the same time, three gazebos were built at the southern end of the rockery. The eastern zigzag walkway was connected with the Phoebe nanmu Hall, and a painted boat-shaped room was built on the west wall of the hall, thus forming a complete courtyard space.

To the east of the Small-Rock Mountain Retreat is the Ancestor Hall of the He family. This hall was originally the place where ancestral tablets were enshrined. The existing Ancestor Hall is a two-storey building and more than ten bungalows with brick and wood structure. The two units in the hall are lined up in separate tracks, each with its own separate courtyard. In the west, there is the Xiangtang Hall, where the ancestors are worshiped. There is a wing in the west that was originally a signing house to manage all kinds of projects. The east is the Qintang Hall, which is the main space of the Ancestral Hall used for preserving images of He's ancestors.

104 片石山房假山与水池-a, 2018年12月
The rockery and the pond in the Small-Rock Mountain Retreat-a, December 2018

105 片石山房假山南立面图
South elevation of the rockery in the Small-Rock Mountain Retreat

106 片石山房假山与水池-b, 2018年12月
The rockery and the pond in the Small-Rock Mountain Retreat-b, December 2018

107　修复片石山房假山时的工地，1989年，陈景贵摄. 来源：扬州何园管理处提供
Construction site for the restoration of the rockery in the Small-Rock Mountain Retreat, 1989, photo by Chen Jinggui. Source: Management Office of Heyuan Garden, Yangzhou

108 片石山房假山及园墙，2018年12月
The rockery in the Small-Rock Mountain Retreat and the garden wall, December 2018

1989年扬州市园林管理部门聘请吴肇钊和孙玉根修复片石山房。修复工作对原有东、西两部分假山遗存给予充分保护，参考石涛的画稿和何家后代的回忆，将片石山房假山东、西两段山体连接起来，形成完整的山水景观。园林专家陈从周先生称之为"细心复笔，画本再全"之作。

The local garden management department invited Wu Zhaozhao and Sun Yugen to restore the artificial mountain of the Small-Rock Mountain Retreat. The restoration fully protected the historical remains of the east and west pieces of the rockery, and connected them to form a completed rockery based on the research of Shitao's paintings and the records from the He family. Chen Congzhou, the master of Chinese classical garden, called this project 'a meticulous "rewriting" and a successful completion based on traditional paintings'.

109 片石山房剖面图
Section of the Small-Rock Mountain Retreat

楠木厅
Phoebe nanmu Hall

舫屋
Boat-shaped room

110 片石山房西立面图
West elevation of the Small-Rock Mountain Retreat

曲廊
Zigzag walkway

111 何家祠堂剖面图
Section of the Ancestor Hall

楠木厅
Phoebe nanmu Hall

祠堂入口
Entrance of the Ancestor Hall

0　　1　　　　5　　　　　　10 m

112 片石山房入口剖面图
Section of the entry of the Small-Rock Mountain Retreat

113 片石山房长廊及门洞剖面图
Section of the corridor and gate in the Small-Rock Mountain Retreat

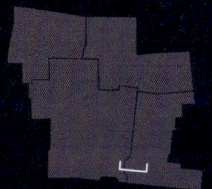

其他区域

经过数十年的努力，何园的主体区域已经逐步收回，并作为文化遗产得到保护。但根据历史考证，目前何园的保护范围仍旧是残缺的。历史上的何园北至刁家巷，东至徐凝门大街，南至花园巷南50米，西至安徽会馆，总面积约50亩（约3.3公顷）。由于产权等因素，一些重要区域至今还未纳入保护范围：一是位于何园东南部的签押房，原为何园主人办公管理用房，随着城市道路改造，目前已经成为沿街商铺；二是位于何园西南侧的西花厅区域，面积约800平方米，现为723所停车场及仓库，而遗存的西花厅已破烂不堪，成为危房；三是位于何园西围墙以西、安徽会馆以东的西园区域，占地面积约为7161平方米，原为何园主人借于李瀚章在扬州的居所，现为723所职工住宅楼和集体宿舍；四是何园南侧花园巷以南的区域，根据1985年航拍影像显示，今天的花园巷向北移动了约20米，这一区域内原为何园各路首进建筑，现作为723所科研用房。此外，由于城市发展过程中缺少建筑高度管控，何园周围出现了一些高大的建筑物，对历史环境风貌和景观视线形成了干扰。目前，当地园林管理部门和相关单位正在不懈努力，以期更好地修复和保护何园。

Other precincts of Heyuan Garden

Although the main area of Heyuan Garden has been recovered following decades of effort, based on historic research, the current conservation area of garden is still incomplete. In the history, Heyuan Garden was north to Diaojia Lane, east to Xuningmen Street, south to 50 metres south from Huayuan Lane, and west to Anhui Guild Hall, with a total area of about 50 *mu* (about 3.3 ha). However, due to issues concerning property rights, the above boundaries have not yet been included in the scope of protection. The first is the signing house located on the southeast side of the current Heyuan Garden, which was the office of the original owner. It has become a street shop after the urban road reconstruction. The second is the Xihua Hall area, located on the southwest side of the current Heyuan Garden. The area is about 800 square metres. It is now the parking lots and warehouses of the Institute 723. The remaining Xihua Hall is now in a dangerous state of ruin. The third is the West Garden area. On the west of the west wall, east of the Anhui Guild Hall, it covers an area of about 7,161 square metres. The owner of the original garden loaned this section to Li Hanzhang as Li's residence in Yangzhou. It is now the residential buildings and the collective dormitory of the Institute 723. The fourth is the southern part of Heyuan Garden. According to the historic research, Huayuan Lane is now 20 metres away from the north. In addition, due to the lack of height restrictions around the Heyuan Garden area during urban development, many of the sights have been disturbed by the surrounding buildings and the historical features have been damaged. At present, the local garden management department and related units have been making significant efforts to restore and protect the garden.

114 何园西南部航拍图, 2019年6月
Aerial photo of the south-western part of Heyuan Garden, June 2019

12 附 录
Appendix

项目团队

研究指导：韩锋
研究负责人：杨晨、李·夏特
研究团队：周宏俊、吴杭彬、庄安頔、郭晓彤、程安祺、林荟

支持单位

同济大学建筑与城市规划学院景观学系
澳大利亚格里菲斯大学工程与建成环境学院
国际古迹遗址理事会–国际风景园林师联合会文化景观科学委员会
江苏省扬州市何园管理处
同济大学建筑设计研究院(集团)有限公司
上海建筑数字建造工程技术研究中心

本书为以下研究基金项目成果

国家自然科学基金青年科学基金项目：基于三维点云数据的遗产景观空间模式识别研究
项目批准号：51608369

同济大学中央高校基本科研业务费专项基金项目：新型测绘技术支持下的遗产景观空间模式识别与可视化
项目批准号：22120180065

同济大学建筑与城市规划学院建成环境技术中心国际开放课题：基于新型测绘技术的风景遗产空间特征识别与可视化研究
项目批准号：2018040301

Project Team

Project Consultant: Han Feng
Director: Yang Chen, Leigh Shutter
Research Team Members: Zhou Hongjun, Wu Hangbin, Zhuang Andi, Guo Xiaotong, Cheng Anqi, Lin Hui

Supporting Institutions

Department of Landscape Architecture, College of Architecture and Urban Planning, Tongji Univeristy
School of Engineering and Built Environment, Griffth University, Australia
ICOMOS-IFLA International Scientific Committee on Cultural Landscapes (ISCCL)
Management Office of Heyuan Garden in Yangzhou, Jiangsu Province
Tongji Architectural Design (Group) Co., Ltd.
Shanghai Digital Architecture Fabrication Engineering Technology Center (SFAB)

This research was supported by the following grants

National Natural Science Foundation of China (Youth Foundation): Research on Spatial Pattern Recognition for Heritage Landscape Using 3D Point Cloud
Grant Number 51608369

Fundamental Research Funds for the Central Universities: Capturing and Visualising Spatial Patterns of Heritage Landscapes Based on Innovative Survey Technologies
Grant Number 22120180065

Research Funds for the International Open Projects in the College of Architecture and Urban Planning (CAUP) in Tongji University: Identification and Visuralisation of the Spatial Character of Landscape Heritage Based on Innovative Survey Technologies
Grant Number 2018040301

图纸目录

插图
1 《富春山居图》（《剩山图》部分）/ 16-17
2 勒内·笛卡尔在《人类论》中绘制的视觉原理图 / 18
3 《巴比伦世界地图》/ 22
4 《三国演义》插图 / 24
5 圣彼得大教堂设计方案木质模型 / 24
6 孔特的雕版机 / 26
7 版画 / 26
8 阿尔布雷特·丢勒的木版画：《鲁特琴的制图员》/ 27
9 伽利略·伽利莱创作的月球视图 / 28
10 美国新墨西哥州的卡尔·詹斯基超大型天线阵 / 30
11 烟草上部叶片表面的扫描电子显微镜图像 / 32
12 木刻《白天和黑夜》/ 33
13 拙政园的虚拟现实体验 / 34
17 中国江苏省扬州市区位 / 53

点云影像
14 上海豫园三维点云扫描模型 / 35
25 何园点云正射影像图 / 70
27 何园北部整体剖面图 / 74-75
28 何园点云模型透视图 / 76-77
29 何园地面高程分析图 / 78
32 园居院落轴测图 / 85
33 园居院落点云正射影像图 / 86
37 何园西部整体剖面图 / 94-95
38 何园中部整体剖面图 / 96-97
39 与归堂立面图 / 98
40 骑马楼立面图 / 98
42 赏月楼与西洋楼立面图 / 100
44 西洋楼北部立面图 / 102
45 西洋楼南部立面图 / 103
46 西洋楼西部立面图 / 104
47 西洋楼东部立面图 / 105

50 赏月楼院落剖面图-a / 108
51 赏月楼院落剖面图-b / 109
52 西园轴测图 / 111
53 西园点云正射影像图 / 112
56 西园透视图 / 118
58 西园底层轴测图 / 120-121
59 西园上层轴测图 / 122-123
60 蝴蝶厅立面图 / 124-125
63 西园剖面图 / 128-129
67 西园南部剖面图 / 134-135
68 西园水心亭剖面图 / 136
69 西园复道回廊立面图-a / 136
70 西园复道回廊立面图-b / 137
71 西园假山剖面图 / 138
77 水心亭透视图 / 144
78 水心亭立面图 / 145
79 东园轴测图 / 147
80 东园点云正射影像图 / 148
84 东园贴壁假山轴测图 / 156-157
85 东园贴壁假山立面图（东段）/ 158-159
86 东园贴壁假山立面图（西段）/ 160-161
87 东园贴壁假山立面图（中段）/ 162-163
91 东园东院立面图 / 168-169
92 东园东院云墙立面图 / 170-171
100 片石山房轴测图 / 181
101 片石山房点云正射影像图 / 182
105 片石山房假山南立面图 / 190-191
109 片石山房剖面图 / 196-197
110 片石山房西立面图 / 198-199
111 何家祠堂剖面图 / 200-201
112 片石山房入口剖面图 / 202
113 片石山房长廊及门洞剖面图 / 203

Figures

Illustrations
1 *Dwelling in the Fuchun Mountains (The Remaining Mountain* scroll) / 16-17
2 Theory of vision from René Descartes' *De Homine* (Treatise on Man) / 18
3 *Imago Mundi* / 22
4 Illustration from *Romance of the Three Kingdoms* / 24
5 Timber model of design proposal St. Peter's Basilica / 24
6 Conté's engraving machine / 26
7 Engraving / 26
8 *The Draftsman of Lute* by Albrecht Dürer / 27
9 Moon view by Galileo Galilei / 28
10 The Karl G. Jansky VLA, New Mexico, USA / 30
11 Scanning electron microscope image of *Nicotiana alata* upper leaf surface / 32
12 *Day and Night*, woodcut / 33
13 Virtual reality experience at Zhuozheng Garden (Humble Administrator Garden) / 34
17 Location of Yangzhou, Jiangsu Province, China / 53

Point cloud images
14 The 3D point cloud scanning model of Yuyuan Garden in Shanghai / 35
25 Orthographic point cloud map of Heyuan Garden / 70
27 The overall section of the northern part of Heyuan Garden / 74-75
28 Point cloud model of Heyuan Garden / 76-77
29 Relative ground levels of Heyuan Garden / 78
32 Isometric of the Residential Yards / 85
33 Orthographic point cloud map of the Residential Yards / 86
37 The overall section of the western part of Heyuan Garden / 94-95
38 The overall section of the middle part of Heyuan Garden / 96-97
39 Elevation of Yugui Hall / 98
40 Elevation of Qima Building / 98
42 Elevation of Shangyue Building and the Western-Style Building / 100
44 North elevation of the Western-Style Building / 102
45 South elevation of the Western-Style Building / 103
46 West elevation of the Western-Style Building / 104
47 East elevation of the Western-Style Building / 105
50 Section-a of Shangyue Building yard / 108
51 Section-b of Shangyue Building yard / 109
52 Isometric of the West Garden / 111
53 Orthographic point cloud map of the West Garden / 112
56 Perspective of the West Garden / 118
58 West Garden lower level isometric / 120-121
59 West Garden upper level isometric / 122-123
60 Elevation of the Butterfly Hall / 124-125
63 Section of the West Garden / 128-129
67 Section of the southern part of the West Garden / 134-135
68 Section of Shuixin Pavilion in the West Garden / 136
69 Elevation-a of the Double-Level Walkway in the West Garden / 136
70 Elevation-b of the Double-Level Walkway in the West Garden / 137
71 Section of the rockery in the West Garden / 138
77 Perspective of Shuixin Pavilion / 144
78 Elevations of Shuixin Pavilion / 145
79 Isometric of the East Garden / 147
80 Orthographic point cloud map of the East Garden / 148
84 East Garden wall rockery isometric / 156-157
85 East Garden wall rockery elevation (east section) / 158-159
86 East Garden wall rockery elevation (west section) / 160-161
87 East Garden wall rockery elevation (middle section) / 162-163
91 Elevation of the east yard of the East Garden / 168-169
92 Section of the cloud-shaped wall in the east yard of the East Garden / 170-171
100 Isometric of the Small-Rock Mountain Retreat / 181
101 Orthographic point cloud map of the Small-Rock Mountain Retreat / 182
105 South elevation of the rockery in the Small-Rock Mountain Retreat / 190-191
109 Section of the Small-Rock Mountain Retreat / 196-197
110 West elevation of the Small-Rock Mountain Retreat / 198-199
111 Section of the Ancestor Hall / 200-201

历史照片

21 何维键全身像 / 60
23 何维键的第四代嫡孙在蝴蝶厅前合影 / 64
48 何维键的曾（外）孙女何祚惠（左）和王承礼在西洋楼合影 / 106
57 水心亭 / 119
61 蝴蝶厅 / 126
65 复道回廊 / 132
74 西园假山与复道回廊 / 141
75 西园水池与水心亭 / 142
88 近月亭 / 164
93 东园门 / 172
96 桴海轩前的石峰和槐树 / 175
97 桴海轩（船厅）/ 176
107 修复片石山房假山时的工地 / 194

现状照片

15 无锡寄畅园 / 40
18 何园航拍图-a / 54-55
20 片石山房太湖石假山 / 58
24 何园航拍图-b / 69
31 何园航拍图-c / 82-83
35 园居院落航拍图-a / 88-89
36 西洋楼内院 / 90
41 园居院落航拍图-b / 99
43 赏月楼立面 / 101
49 西洋楼外廊 / 107
55 西园航拍图 / 114-115
62 蝴蝶厅 / 127
64 复道回廊内景 / 130-131
66 复道回廊 / 133
72 西园湖石假山主峰 / 139
73 西园假山与复道回廊 / 140
76 西园水池与水心亭 / 143
82 东园航拍图-a / 150-151
83 东园航拍图-b / 154-155
89 近月亭 / 165
90 东园航拍图-c / 166-167
94 东园门 / 173
95 桴海轩前的石峰和槐树 / 174
98 桴海轩（船厅）/ 177
99 牡丹厅东山墙上的"凤吹牡丹"砖雕 / 178-179
103 片石山房航拍图 / 184-185
104 片石山房假山与水池-a / 188-189
106 片石山房假山与水池-b / 192-193
108 片石山房假山及园墙 / 195
114 何园西南部航拍图 / 206-207

地图与图解

16 拙政园平面图 / 44
19 扬州古城区古典园林分布图 / 57
22 何园范围的演变 / 62-63
26 何园一层平面图 / 71
30 何园园林要素格局分析 / 80-81
34 园居院落一层平面图 / 87
54 西园一层平面图 / 113
81 东园一层平面图 / 149
102 片石山房一层平面图 / 183

注：本书中未标明出处的图片均为作者自制、自摄或自绘。

- 112 Section of the entry of the Small-Rock Mountain Retreat / 202
- 113 Section of the corridor and gate in the Small-Rock Mountain Retreat / 203

Historic photos
- 21 He Weijian portrait / 60
- 23 He Weijian's great-grandsons in front of the Butterfly Hall, 1935 / 64
- 48 He Zuohui (left) and Wang Chengli, the great-granddaughters of He Weijian in front of the Western-Style Building / 106
- 57 Shuixin Pavilion / 119
- 61 The Butterfly Hall / 126
- 65 The Double-Level Walkway / 132
- 74 The rockery and the Double-Level Walkway in the West Garden / 141
- 75 The pond and Shuixin Pavilion in the West Garden / 142
- 88 Jinyue Pavilion / 164
- 93 Gate of the East Garden / 172
- 96 Rock and pagoda tree in front of Fuhai Hall / 175
- 97 Fuhai Hall (the Boat Hall) / 176
- 107 Construction site for the restoration of the rockery in the Small-Rock Mountain Retreat / 194

Contemporary photos
- 15 Jichang Garden (Solace-Imbued Garden) in Wuxi / 40
- 18 Aerial photo-a of Heyuan Garden / 54-55
- 20 Taihu Lake stone rockery in the Small-Rock Mountain Retreat / 58
- 24 Aerial photo-b of Heyuan Garden / 69
- 31 Aerial photo-c of Heyuan Garden / 82-83
- 35 Aerial photo-a of the Residential Yards / 88-89
- 36 Courtyard of the Western-Style Building / 90
- 41 Aerial photo-b of the Residential Yards / 99
- 43 Shangyue Building / 101
- 49 The veranda of the Western-Style Building / 107
- 55 Aerial photo of the West Garden / 114-115
- 62 The Butterfly Hall / 127
- 64 Interior of the Double-Level Walkway / 130-131
- 66 The Double-Level Walkway / 133
- 72 The peak of the rockery in the West Garden / 139
- 73 The rockery and the Double-Level Walkway in the West Garden / 140
- 76 The pond and Shuixin Pavilion in the West Garden / 143
- 82 Aerial photo-a of the East Garden / 150-151
- 83 Aerial photo-b of the East Garden / 154-155
- 89 Jinyue Pavilion / 165
- 90 Aerial photo-c of the East Garden / 166-167
- 94 Gate of the East Garden / 173
- 95 The rock and pagoda tree in front of Fuhai Hall / 174
- 98 Fuhai Hall (the Boat Hall) / 177
- 99 The phoenix and peony brick carving embedded in the east gable of Mudan Hall / 178-179
- 103 Aerial photo of the Small-Rock Mountain Retreat / 184-185
- 104 The rockery and the pond in the Small-Rock Mountain Retreat-a / 188-189
- 106 The rockery and the pond in the Small-Rock Mountain Retreat-b / 192-193
- 108 The rockery in the Small-Rock Mountain Retreat and the garden wall / 195
- 114 Aerial photo of the south-western part of Heyuan Garden / 206-207

Maps and diagrams
- 16 Plan of Zhuozheng Garden (Humble Administrator Garden) / 44
- 19 The classical gardens in the historic town of Yang zhou / 57
- 22 The evolution of the boundary of Heyuan Garden / 62-63
- 26 Ground floor plan of Heyuan Garden / 71
- 30 Feature analysis of Heyuan Garden / 80-81
- 34 Ground floor plan of the Residential Yards / 87
- 54 Ground floor plan of the West Garden / 113
- 81 Ground floor plan of the East Garden / 149
- 102 Ground floor plan of the Small-Rock Mountain Retreat / 183

Note: The figures without the indication of sources are all made by the authors.

参考书目
Bibliography

陈从周. 苏州园林. 上海: 同济大学建筑系印刷, 同济大学教材科出版, 1956.

陈从周. 扬州园林. 上海: 同济大学出版社, 2007.

陈从周. 中国文人园林. 北京: 外语教学与研究出版社, 2018.

尼古拉·尼葛洛庞帝. 数字化生存. 胡泳, 范海燕, 译. 北京: 电子工业出版社, 2017.

李斗. 扬州画舫录. 北京: 中华书局, 1960.

童寯. 江南园林志（第二版）（典藏版）. 北京: 中国建筑工业出版社, 2014.

王虎华, 王海燕. 何园志. 南京: 南京师范大学出版社, 2017.

王其亨. 古建筑测绘. 北京: 中国建筑工业出版社, 2006.

许少飞. 扬州园林史话. 扬州: 广陵书社, 2014.

《扬州市园林志》编纂委员会. 扬州市园林志. 扬州: 广陵书社, 2018.

周维权. 中国古典园林史. 2版. 北京: 清华大学出版社, 1999.

朱江. 扬州园林品赏录. 上海: 上海文化出版社, 1984.

Akerman, James R., and Robert W. Karrow. Maps: Finding Our Place in the World. Chicago: University of Chicago Press, 2007.

Bastéa, Eleni. Memory and Architecture. Albuquerque: University of New Mexico Press, 2004.

Berger, John. Ways of Seeing. New York: Viking Press, 1973.

Bowler, Peter J., and Iwan Rhys Morus. Making Modern Science: A Historical Survey. Chicago: University of Chicago Press, 2005.

Cosgrove, Denis Edmund, eds. Mappings (Critical Views). London: Reaktion Books, 1999.

Cosgrove, Denis Edmund. Geographical Imagination and the Authority of Images: Hettner-Lecture with Denis Cosgrove. Stuttgart: Steiner, 2006.

Cosgrove, Denis Edmund. Geography and Vision: Seeing, Imagining and Representing the World. London: I.B. Tauris, 2008.

Cosgrove, Denis E., and Stephen Daniels. The Iconography of Landscape: Essays on the Symbolic Representation, Design and Use of Past Environments. U.K: Cambridge University Press, 1992.

Cresswell, Tim. Place: A Short Introduction. Malden, MA: Blackwell, 2004.

Desimini, Jill, and Charles Waldheim. Cartographic Grounds: Projecting the Landscape Imaginary. New York: Princeton Architectural Press, 2016.

Edgerton, David. The Shock of the Old: Technology and Global History since 1900. London: Profile Books, 2019.

Ferdinand, Simon. Mapping beyond Measure: Art, Cartography, and the Space of Global Modernity. Lincoln: University of Nebraska Press, 2019.

Finnane, Antonia. Speaking of Yangzhou: A Chinese City, 1550–1850. Cambridge (Massachusetts) and London: Published by the Harvard University Asia Centre and distributed by Harvard University Press, 2004.

Heise, Ursula. Sense of Place and Sense of Planet: The Environmental Imagination of the Global. Oxford: Oxford University Press, 2008.

International Council of Monuments and Sites (ICOMOS). Principles for the Recording of Monuments, Groups of Buildings and Sites. Paris, France: International Council of Monuments and Sites, 1996.

Mirzoeff, Nicholas. How to See the World. London: Pelican, 2014.

Nagel, Thomas. The View from Nowhere. New York; Oxford: Oxford University Press, 1986.

Rouse, Joseph. Articulating the World: Conceptual Understanding and the Scientific Image. Chicago: The University of Chicago Press, 2015.

Tuan, Yi-Fu. Space and Place: The Perspective of Experience. Minneapolis: University of Minnesota Press, 1977

Tuan, Yi-fu. Topophilia: A Study of Environmental Perception, Attitudes, and Values. New York: Columbia University Press, 1990.

Tuan, Yi-fu, and Tammy Mercure. Place, Art, and Self. Santa Fe, N.M.; Staunton, Va.: Center for American Places in association with Columbia College Distributed by the University of Virginia Press, 2004.

Turchi, Peter. Maps of the Imagination: The Writer as Cartographer. San Antonio, Texas: Trinity University Press, 2004.

UNESCO. The Convention for the Safeguarding of Intangible Cultural Heritage. Paris, France: UNESCO, 2003.

UNESCO. Recommendation on the Historic Urban Landscape. In Records of the General Conference 36th session. Paris, France: UNESCO, 2011.

作者信息

杨晨

杨晨博士现任同济大学建筑与城市规划学院助理教授，硕士生导师，国际文化遗产档案委员会（CIPA）专家委员，国际古迹遗址理事会－国际风景园林师联合会文化景观科学委员会专家委员、数字化文化景观工作小组共同召集人，中国风景园林学会文化景观专业委员会副秘书长。杨晨博士主要致力于数字化遗产景观方向的理论研究与保护实践，先后主持国家公派博士项目、国家自然科学基金青年科学基金项目，参与国家重点研发计划项目、上海市哲学社会科学规划课题。2016年起在同济大学开设"数字化遗产景观"全英文本科课程，2018年获得西澳大学高级访问学者基金。

李·夏特

李·夏特先生是格里菲斯大学工程与建成环境学院建筑与设计系副教授。他拥有建筑学本科和硕士学位，也是澳大利亚皇家建筑师学会成员、注册建筑师。夏特副教授是格里菲斯大学建筑学硕士学位项目负责人，也是格里菲斯设计与创新研究中心人居实验室主任。他拥有16年的全职教师经验和超过35年的注册建筑师实践经验，曾在澳大利亚、中国、日本和美国等国家开展建筑设计，并在布里斯班创立了星球设计合作建筑设计公司。李·夏特副教授的建筑实践和学术研究主要聚焦于集成研究，即持续不断地积极开展面向应用的创新实践、教学和研究。近年来他的工作主要集中在利用新型三维测绘和图示技术保护城市文化遗产。2018年，他被聘为同济大学兼职科研专家。

About the authors

Yang Chen

Dr. Yang Chen is an Assistant Professor and Masters student supervisor in the College of Architecture and Urban Planning (CAUP) at Tongji University. He is also an expert member of CIPA Heritage Documentation, a contributing member of the ICOMOS-IFLA International Scientific Committee on Cultural Landscapes (co-convenor of the Digital Cultural Landscape Working Group), and the Deputy Secretary General of the Chinese Society of Landscape Architecture Cultural Landscape Committee. His research has focused on the digital conservation, management and interpretation of heritage landscapes in different cultural contexts. He has participated in or presided over some important research projects on digital heritage landscapes, including China Scholarship Council project, National Natural Science Foundation, National Key Research and Development Plan, and Shanghai Philosophy and Social Sciences Planning Project, etc. Dr. Yang obtained the Advanced Studies Visiting Fellowships from the University of Western Australia in 2018. In Tongji University, he set up the first undergraduate course entitled Digital Heritage Landscape in 2016.

Leigh Shutter

Leigh Shutter [BArch, MSc (Arch & Bldg Des), FRAIA, QLD Reg Arch 2903] is an Associate Professor in the Architecture and Design programs in the School of Engineering and Built Environment at Griffith University. He is Program Director for the Master of Architecture degree and Head of the Human Habitats Lab at the Griffith Centre for Design and Innovation Research. He has been a full time academic for 16 years and a practicing registered architect for over 35 years, working in and leading architectural practices in Australia, China, Japan and the United States. He was the founding principal of the Brisbane-based architectural practice Planet Design Collaborative. Associate Professor Shutter's architectural and academic career has focused on integrated scholarship: an ongoing and active participation in innovative application oriented practice, teaching and research. In recent years this work has focused on the application of new 3D survey and mapping technologies with a particular focus on urban cultural heritage. In 2018, he was appointed as a Visiting Professorial Research Fellow at Tongji University.

图书在版编目（CIP）数据

数字化园林遗产图录：扬州何园 = Garden Heritage Digital Document: Heyuan Garden / Yangzhou：汉英对照 / 杨晨，(澳) 李·夏特 (Leigh Shutter) 著. -- 上海：同济大学出版社，2020.6

ISBN 978-7-5608-8932-0

Ⅰ. ①数… Ⅱ. ①杨… ②李… Ⅲ. ①古典园林—文化遗产—数字化—扬州—图录 Ⅳ. ①K928.73

中国版本图书馆CIP数据核字(2019)第288755号

联合国教科文组织世界遗产中国项目研究
世界遗产与文化景观·数字档案系列
丛书主编：韩锋
Research Projects on UNESCO World Heritage in China
World Heritage and Cultural Landscapes — Digital Documentation Series
Editor-in-Chief: Han Feng

数字化园林遗产图录：扬州何园
Garden Heritage Digital Document: Heyuan Garden / Yangzhou

杨晨　[澳]李·夏特 著
Yang Chen, Leigh Shutter

出 版 人	华春荣
策　　划	江岱
责任编辑	朱笑黎
责任校对	徐春莲
书籍设计	杨　晨　李·夏特
封面设计	徐文馨
出版发行	同济大学出版社　www.tongjipress.com.cn
	（地址：上海市四平路1239号　邮编：200092　电话：021-65985622）
经　　销	全国各地新华书店
印　　刷	上海安枫印务有限公司
开　　本	787mm×1092mm　1/12
印　　张	18
字　　数	454 000
版　　次	2020年6月第1版　2020年6月第1次印刷
书　　号	ISBN 978-7-5608-8932-0
定　　价	188元

本书若有印装质量问题，请向本社发行部调换
版权所有 侵权必究

ISBN 978-7-5608-8932-0
Publisher: Hua Chunrong
Initiated by: Jiang Dai
Editor: Zhu Xiaoli
Proofreading: Xu Chunlian
Book Design: Yang Chen, Leigh Shutter
Book Cover Design: Xu Wenxin
Published in June 2020, by Tongji University Press,
1239, Siping Road, Shanghai, China, 200092
www.tongjipress.com.cn

All rights reserved